THE LOVE CURE

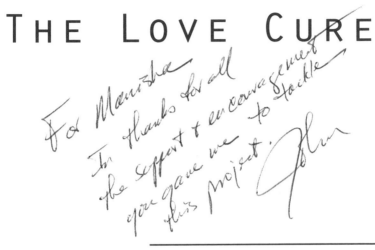

*For Manisha,
In thanks for all
the support + encouragement
you gave me to tackle
this project.*
John

THERAPY EROTIC AND SEXUAL

JOHN RYAN HAULE

Spring Publications, Inc.
Woodstock, Connecticut

Published by Spring Publications, Inc., 299 East Quassett Road, Woodstock, CT 06281, e-mail: spring@neca.com. Text printed on acid-free paper.
First printing 1996. Cover and text design by Brian O'Kelley.

Library of Congress Cataloging-in-Publication Data

Haule, John R., 1942-
      The love cure : therapy erotic and sexual / John Ryan Haule.
      p.   cm. — (Jungian classics series ; 13)
      Includes bibliographic references.
      ISBN 0-88214-513-4 (alk. paper)
      1. Psychotherapy—Erotic aspects. 2. Psychotherapist and patient. 3. Love. I. Title II. Series.
      RC489.E75H38   1996
      616.89 ' 14—dc20   96-7013
                                                                CIP

 PRINTED IN CANADA

For John T. Dillon, who got me started on this path

Acknowledgments

Aside from all the people—therapists, patients, and friends—who have taught me the nature of erotic interaction by being themselves and valuing me, I would like particularly to thank Manisha Roy for repeatedly urging me to write this book. Thanks to her and Lena Ross, as well, for publishing the first article in which I broached the issues which are developed here. I am grateful to Toni Frey and Roger Brooke for encouraging my phenomenological interests and to Cecile Tougas for showing me what it means to "shout" phenomenologically. I thank Peter Rutter, too, for his book, *Sex in the Forbidden Zone*. His intelligent and compassionate argument and examples represent what is not discussed here, as this book takes up what he left out.

Contents

Introduction	Framing Eros	9
One	Erotic Therapy and the Shape of Eros	19
Two	Where Are Our Boundaries?	36
Three	Eros and Union	55
Four	The Love Cure Part I *The Love They Had Longed for as Children*	82
Five	The Love Cure Part II *If No Bond of Love Exists, They Have No Soul*	99
Six	Therapy and Sex	118
Seven	The Ethics of the Love Cure	137
Eight	Marrying the Patient	154
Conclusion	Frustration, Optimal and Depreciating	164
Appendix	Summary of the Argument	169
Bibliography		175

Framing Eros

Most essays on therapy, Eros, and sex, are treatises on what one should do or not do, and why. This one is not. My aim is to open up a way of seeing.

Psychotherapy today is dominated officially by an image of its work borrowed from medicine. The patient is to be diagnosed correctly as suffering from a certain disease entity (such as pneumonia), and the disease itself will determine the mode of therapy (e.g., antibiotics and bed rest). In this model of illness the person of the patient and the person of the doctor are entirely irrelevant. The disease is an invading organism or structural dysfunction that can be addressed in isolation from the individuals involved or their relationship.

Insurance companies insist upon this way of seeing psychotherapy because it gives them a sense that they know what to expect in paying for a recovery process. A certain disease entity, defined in accordance with the categories of the *Diagnostic and Statistical Manual of Mental Disorders*, may be expected to require a certain number of visits to a practitioner who follows a certain predicted course of action. If the results are not as predictable with "anxiety disorder" as they are with "coronary thrombosis," it may be that the therapist is less than fully competent.

Psychotherapists are nervous with this kind of model, for it expects clear results in an area of dismal unclarity. Nevertheless it appears we are flattered to be seen as capable of the scientific kind of respectability that is accorded the medical profession's approach to physical disease. And we are delighted to receive payment.

This commending picture of therapy as a scientific technique for curing disease and repairing the disturbed mechanics of the psyche clashes dramatically with what people *say* about their therapists. They speak of how engaging, boring, wise, inspiring, sympathetic, stern, or dense they may be. And therapists, for our part, refer to our patients in similar language, as exciting, challenging, trying, demanding, and the like.

Psychotherapy is experienced as a human relationship of central importance in people's lives. Our relationships with our therapists and patients are definitive for how we see ourselves and how we change. We speak of "transference," meaning the nimbus of authority a patient ascribes to a therapist, and of "countertransference," the equally powerful emotional reaction of the therapist to the patient. While there is always a transference and countertransference of some kind, the particular form they take is unique in each case and determined by the personalities involved. Patients are shamed and elated as they find themselves falling in love with their therapists, and therapists are no less affected in return.

Therapy seems to be an *erotic* encounter when we pay attention to these informal testimonies. But it is dangerous to think so, in these days when sexual abuse is so much on our minds and when the newspapers are filled with accounts of therapists who have "violated their trust" and initiated affairs with their patients.

Eros is the Greek god of attraction, who was revered for his bringing people together in friendship and community. But he is also the god of sexuality. Erotic love, from the Greek word, *eros*, designates a passionate and tempestuous entanglement between people. Strictly speaking, sexuality is not implied by the love the Greeks called *eros*, but we no longer make that distinction clearly. We speak of erotic dress, erotic stories, and erotic pictures, meaning that they are charged with compelling and even vulgar sexuality.

Framing Eros

Because Eros inspires such an "unscientific" emotion, we are reluctant to say that therapy is an erotic enterprise. Eros has been "framed." Although guilty of no crime himself, he has been hanging out with questionable associates, and the circumstantial evidence does not look good. If we call therapy "erotic," people may think we mean it is "sexual" or that we advocate sexual misconduct by therapists. Because "the erotic" is so thoroughly confused with "the sexual," people think they know who Eros is, even though they have hardly made his acquaintance.

This book reframes the questions we ask about Eros and therapy. If Eros draws people together to build communities and cities, he is a god who inspires interest and passion, who gets us involved, who reveals to us the emotional value and meaning of the enterprises that engage us. We might begin by asking what does Eros *feel* like? What does he *do* to us? What is he trying to achieve?

If therapy engages us in a work of compelling interest, if it binds us together as people who mean something to one another, is Eros not present? Is he a welcome guest? Does he come and go? Does he help the process, hinder it, or both together?

What would therapy look like if we framed it as an essentially *erotic* enterprise? What would that bring to light about the therapeutic process? Does it mean the therapist would be expected to *love* her patient? Can love ever be "expected?" If she does love her patient, does this make her a kind of mother or mistress? Would that not be "regressive?" Is this why therapists fall in love with their patients? How might a therapist "love" in a "therapeutic" manner? Is there anything therapeutic about love, or should all forms of love be left outside the professional contract observed by patient and therapist?

Nearly a hundred years ago, Freud defined certain therapeutic processes as an "analyzing" of the "transference neurosis."[1] He meant that the patient's neurosis has so structured his life that he turns every occasion into a demonstration of his neurotic point of view and mode of behavior. Therapy itself is such an occasion, and the person of the

---

[1] Jung first introduced the term "transference neurosis" in 1907, to describe neuroses in which the patient's transference to the doctor was of prime importance. Freud developed its meaning as a therapeutic repetition of the patient's more general neurosis in 1914.

therapist is converted by her patient's neurotic lens into one of the significant people (mother, lover, etc.) populating his neurotic lifeworld. The interaction of therapy, therefore, repeats and exemplifies the general form of the neurosis, and the therapist's job is to reveal this structure, piece-by-piece, by means of accurate interpretations made at well-chosen moments when the patient is prepared to accept and understand them.

Thus psychoanalysis proposes a way of seeing therapy. Neurosis is an interpersonal phenomenon that manifests within the interactions between people. The patient has become neurotic because some of his earliest and most influential relationships were distorted and made neurotic by the inadequacies of parents and guardians who first interacted with him; and these became the building blocks with which he has constructed the neurotic universe which he re-establishes in every encounter of his life.

Therapy, too, is an interpersonal interaction, but one that does not simply unfold in a passive and unconscious manner. Surely it is unconscious in part, for this is the means by which the patient unwittingly turns the therapy into another instance of his general neurosis. But the therapist is charged with the responsibility of making these developments conscious so that the neurotic structure can be perceived for what it is—one world construction among many that are possible, and a rather poor one at that.

Neurosis is therefore a way of seeing the world and other people, and therapy is a way of challenging the inevitability of a neurotic mode of seeing. It does not work like an antibiotic to kill invading organisms nor like a cast to hold broken bones in place while they reknit. It engages the world-constructing intelligent and emotional faculties of the patient through an interaction with the corresponding faculties of the therapist. Two people encounter one another where they respectively live—in mind, heart, and soul. Their interchanges move both of them vitally, so much so that they become highly important in one another's lives.

If the patient complains primarily of the disappointments and disasters in her love life, the therapist is inevitably drawn into a consideration of his own relationships, satisfying and unsatisfying. The patient's pain engages her therapist's pain, her poorly defended wounds call out to his perhaps better integrated vulnerabilities. If she complains of her sense of futility, inadequacy, and emptiness, he will be reminded of his own. If he cannot respond out of a personal acquaintance with her pain as a familiar experience in his own life, she is not likely to find him insightful, sympathetic, or understanding. She will not feel "met." Furthermore, if he cannot encounter her pain and impotence as something he has learned to transform into sensitivity, growth, and renewal in his own life, she will soon feel stuck with him in a common morass.

Beyond the issue of emotional resonance, therapy as a deeply interpersonal process of "analyzing the transference neurosis" actually calls for the restructuring of the patient's lifeworld. This is a highly intimate undertaking. The patient, in actual fact, has to allow the therapist into the most personal and private reaches of her life, to see and understand what makes her world the unique and vital project it is. Furthermore, the therapist does not just walk along the paths and explore the topography of her soulscape, he also questions its landmarks in a critical and "analytic" way. She allows him to see who she is in the most intimate manner and to effect changes in the way she experiences herself and her world. She exposes the most touchy and embarrassing details of her innermost being.

She is hardly going to allow such intimacy to anyone at all, but only to one who appreciates and respects what he is being permitted to share. She will look to *his* deepest reality—in a very unconscious and intuitive manner, no doubt—but with a skeptical and anxious eye to see how he values and receives her.

She is going to be ready to pull up the drawbridge over the moat of their individual differences at the slightest hint that his clumsiness and insensitivity are incapable of valuing what he sees. He may call this "resistance," and it may very well be; but if he cannot respect her resistances and her doubts about his worthiness to enter so intimate a realm, he does indeed prove himself unworthy.

Thus he enters not at all as a dispassionate and objective observer, but as a participant in her life. His sensitivities are exposed, and with them his own intimate reaches. The interaction we are describing is a meeting of two lifeworlds. His, too, is exposed to her possibly frightened gaze. He reveals himself in every reaction, whether deliberate or unwitting, that he makes to her. Very likely he does not expose his deepest intimacy by revealing the facts of his biography and on-going experiences outside of their interaction, as she does.

No "anamnesis" is required of him—certainly it would be for the most part inappropriate. But such intimate realms as she exposes cannot be entered without personal and immediate exposure. His embarrassments, elations, depressions, distaste, familiarity, and the like, cannot be hidden. Perhaps she has no words to name these reactions of his, but she sees them all the same, and they have profound effects upon her experience of him and her judgment as to whether he can be trusted to continue these explorations.

Although there is not necessarily anything overtly sexual about such intimacies, it would not be inapt to compare them to the "letting in" and sense of privacy that attend the sexual realm. Ironically it seems that very many people are unable to allow their sexual partners such profound access to their innermost personal experience. They may be unable to share their most private fantasies or to tell their spouse precisely what kinds of caresses are the most exciting and enjoyable. These things are felt to be so private and close to shame that many people spend their whole sexual lives without making such confessions and invitations to the person we would expect to be the closest and most trusted.

If such intimacies may not be permitted to a spouse, how much more must we appreciate the kind of trust and respect demanded of a therapeutic relationship between two deeply exposed individuals, one of whom is asking for her lifeworld to be seen for the deeply personal reality it is, to have it respected and valued, and especially to have it criticized and restructured. What could draw them so deeply, fascinatedly, and trustingly into one another, if not a passionate, involving love like that of Eros? If Eros does this, he must be the essential participant in any therapeutic interaction that works to explore and restructure a lifeworld.

In order to appreciate therapy in these terms, we require an adequate and detailed understanding of human meetings as erotic enterprises. We need a much clearer idea of who Eros is and what he effects when two individuals encounter one another at this deeply intimate level. Chapter One takes up this central question and sketches the *structure of erotic interaction* as it manifests generally and in the work of therapy. Appreciating the work of Eros enables us to grasp more fully what happens between therapist and patient when they are drawn to one another, how they defend against it, and what the "sexualizing" of lust does to this encounter.

Chapter Two examines the metaphor of "boundaries," today's most common category for dealing "safely" with erotic feelings in therapy. A therapeutic relationship that turned into a sexual affair is examined in minute detail. Some seventeen meanings of "boundary" are elucidated, and all are shown to have implications that subvert the central aims of therapy and the needs of the patient.

Chapter Three returns to the theme of Eros to describe the pull toward union experienced in erotic interaction, employing the testimony of several Christian mystics regarding what is possible and may be expected of interpersonal union. These are then applied to the therapeutic interaction, which is also shown to harbor a unitive dimension of great power. The chapter ends with a number of questions about the relationship between the unitive moment of therapy and that of sexuality. Eros appears to be the ground and life of therapy, but nothing has been said about therapy's goal.

Chapters Four and Five take up the nature of therapy; and based upon the testimony of Freud, Jung, and Kohut, therapy is found to be essentially a "love cure." Therapeutic love is called "empathy," which has both a unitive moment (the bond between two selves) and a distancing moment whereby the emerging or unfolding self of the patient is seen, appreciated, and articulated accurately. Inevitable frustrations to the patient's sense of self are dealt with empathically, too. The goal of therapy is the "structuring of an emerging self" and the "unfolding of a self" that has already demonstrated adequate coherence.

Chapter Six returns to the problem of sexuality. If the love cure is an erotic engagement, and "the erotic" is hopelessly confused with "the sexual" in the public mind, how may we assure ourselves that the love cure will not become a sexual enactment of the unitive moment in Eros? Because the love cure takes its guidance solely from the emerging or unfolding self of the patient, it cannot accept rules that precede the encounter with that unique individual. Therefore, the question of sexuality has to be left open in principle.

Chapter Seven concerns the open question of sexuality in the context of therapy and articulates the ethical parameters that emerge organically from the nature of the love cure itself. Here it is seen that leaving open the question of sexuality forces therapist and patient to deal with an immense array of issues, many of which would have been prematurely closed had the issue of sexual enactment not been left open. In the process of outlining them, the nature of the love cure is revealed in greater detail. An ethically justified sexual expression in the context of therapy is nearly impossible, and complex ethical demands arise in every moment of the therapeutic interaction. The love-cure therapist is not relieved of responsibility but accepts an even greater burden.

Chapter Eight takes up the rather specialized question of marrying the patient, in order to show that the meaning of this, too, is determined by the way we see the therapeutic endeavor—as well as by how we see marriage.

Erotic love has been the central concern of my work for the past decade. I began with what I thought would be an introduction to the issues of transference and countertransference by writing about human romantic love in general. This project took on a life of its own and eventually was published as its own book, *Divine Madness: Archetypes of Romantic Love* (1990). The material came not only from my personal and clinical experience, but also from novels, tales, mystical documents from the world's religions, and the like. It forms the foundation for all that has followed.

As I searched for a way to apply these discoveries to the therapeutic interchange, I fell back on my own autobiography as a therapist. *Bushwhacking Through Narcissism* (still unpublished) is an account of how my errors and bumbling as a therapist have led me from a classically Jungian interest in dream analysis to a realization of the erotic realities that lie beneath the surface of a traditional approach to therapy. Upon finishing the manuscript, I still had not found a way to address the erotic issues in therapy in the form of a general theory.

What firmed up my perspective was reading Peter Rutter's book, *Sex in the Forbidden Zone* (1989). This very reasonable and clinically astute, even compassionate, treatment of the subject of "sexual acting out" in the context of therapy upset me by what it failed to discuss. I found no appreciation of the profoundly transformative significance of Eros and sexuality in the book, even though the many wonderful examples Rutter provides call out for a deeper interpretation.

I realized as I read Rutter's book that sex is the sticking point in our contemporary understanding of therapy; and as long as it is seen in a purely negative and destructive light, Eros itself lies under a cloud of unexamined suspicion. The "framing" of Eros, in the sense of holding it guilty for everything that goes wrong in therapy, calls out for a different kind of framing. How can erotic feelings be "framed" more usefully in order to understand how they are present in every therapy and hold the secret of therapy's success as well as its failure?

This book answers this question and the others listed above. In doing so, it stakes out a dangerous and controversial turf. Some readers may be enraged that I insist upon opening issues that "ought" to be closed and safely tucked away. Readers of the manuscript who were sympathetic to the topic reported feeling a great deal of anxiety midway through some of the chapters. They felt the dangers of Eros and feared I had not erected sufficient defenses against them.

Deep interpersonal involvement is always dangerous. It is where everyone gets hurt, inevitably. Parents and children, lovers, mentors and students, therapists and patients, every vital pairing in our lives is fraught with the likelihood of injury. Eros dominates a field of elation, pain, and growth—almost the only field in which our development as persons is possible.

We will never come to understand therapy or any powerful human relationship by soft-pedaling the role of Eros. The only sensible approach is to examine our erotic life more closely. This alone will lead to a more adequate understanding of how we live our lives and what role therapy may play in them.

One

Erotic Therapy
and the Shape of Eros

Recently the *Boston Globe* ran a front-page article on sexual misconduct by psychiatrists beginning with an anecdote in which a certain Dr. Mathews struggles to define his feelings for a patient with whom he has been sexually involved for several weeks: "You're not my sister, wife, mother, another friend, daughter. Who are you? My special lover?" The unidentified journalist observes, "He might have tried the truth—victim." Evidently the writer of the article had not a clue to the psychiatrist's emotional befuddlement, for it was treated as a prime example of a male therapist's mendacious arrogance. Meanwhile he was unable to appreciate the damage he may have done. In emotionally charged matters of this kind, the opposing sides pass one another again and again like two ships in the night, orienting themselves by entirely different sets of coordinates.

The individuality of both parties is lost when we speak in collective generalities. On one side the journalist speaks the language of what Jung calls "collective consciousness"—what I prefer to call the "persona field," for it conforms itself to what "everybody knows," formulates into codes, and brandishes as self-righteous slogans: "boundary violation," "power differential," "dual relationship," and "acting out." There is a great deal of truth in the persona field, despite the blindness of its nocturnal course. My caring and conscientious colleague Peter Rutter has articulated its wisdom in his book, *Sex in the Forbidden Zone* (Rutter, 1989), although the publisher's blurb on the cover of the paperback edition also points to its great flaw: "Provocative . . . says all the right things." There is much to be learned from Rutter's book about how sexual involvement by therapists, physicians, teachers, and clergymen with their patients, students, and parishioners is based upon the woundedness and unconsciousness of both parties. He intelligently spells out the bad faith strategies on both sides. But the book is oriented entirely by the coordinates of the persona field.

Dr. Mathews, benighted though he may be, pours over a different map and calculates the angles of different stars. From the perspective of what "everyone knows," he is a cynical manipulator, a pitiful neurotic, or both. He stammers out his sister-wife-mother reply to an unreported question, for he is by no means ignorant of the persona field. He has lived most of his life in the world of public consensus, feels the force of its opinions like a great surging river he has little hope of resisting, and therefore has protected his numinous and illicit affair in careful silence. Nevertheless he has generally not felt himself isolated in quirky idiosyncrasy. His naive stumbling prose "says all the right things" from the collective world of the archetypes where primal truths have stood unchallenged for millennia rather than decades. In the collective unconscious, where *his* ego has dissolved, his patient/lover embodies all of womankind and very likely goddesshood as well. On being accused of sexual predation, he is flabbergasted. How could his supremely true and worshipful love be so miscast?

The opposing parties live in complete and absolute worlds, wholly separate, speaking non-cognate languages. From his vantage atop Mt. Olympus, Dr. Mathews hears his accusers as though they are speaking of the habits of monkeys in the Amazonian rainforest. The journalist listens to him as though he were describing life on Venus. Both Venus and the Amazon, however, belong to the full range of human life. Of his near-death experience, for example, Jung tells us he was so enthralled by the "garden of pomegranates" where he witnessed the wedding of the gods, that he could hardly bear to return "to the gray world with its boxes." (Jung, 1961, p. 295). What is common sense for one, is gray boxes for another. Even those who have studied the language of their opponents—Jungian analysts, for instance—often seem unable to resist the mesmerizing pull to evaluate the transcendent realities of Venus in monkey terms or to throw out common sense with the empty cartons.

Pamela Donleavy, who had been a patient in an erotically charged and successful therapy, chides Rutter for ignoring the collective unconscious in his account of the "forbidden zone." She describes the transformation of the sexual field she shared with her analyst through what she calls (citing Robert Stein) the Pan/Nymph archetype. (Donleavy, 1995).

Donleavy is distressed by Rutter's argument that erotic attraction between client and therapist should be viewed primarily as a danger to be dealt with by flight. She reads Rutter as I do, as recommending that the therapist has an obligation to cordon off the erotic field as counter to the aims of therapy. She argues that her own experience contradicts this. Her therapist did not flee, and she is grateful that he helped her to work through her erotic issues and come to understand herself in terms of the "Pan/Nymph archetype." Rutter, who is a Jungian analyst and therefore trained in the understanding of archetypal psychology, might be expected to agree with her. But he does not. For Rutter archetypes are nothing but landmines in the persona field. He uses the word *myth* repeatedly in his book, but always to mean dangerous and deceptive untruth.

Individuation, as Jung repeatedly makes clear, involves hewing a course of personal integrity *between* the two collectivities, deeply cognizant of the realities of each but seduced by neither. This is explicitly the theme of Jung's most basic and accessible work, *Two Essays in Analytical Psychology*. (Jung, 1966). It is regrettable to think that individuation may not be relevant to the "forbidden zone." A Jungian analyst who writes about these matters while eschewing all mention of the archetypal field may be suspected of being in flight from Eros.

Again we are faced with the specter of ships passing in the night.

As a start toward building a commonality of discourse, I offer some preliminary reflections on the phenomenology of the erotic as we encounter it every day in the hope that they will be sufficiently fundamental to win the acceptance of both sides in the debate. To some degree, whenever we speak of "the erotic," we refer to Eros. But even the Greeks did not name the same psychic force every time they invoked the god. In the earliest texts he is the Son of Chaos and represents the attractive force behind friendships, marriages, and the creation of cities. Later he is the Son of Aphrodite and embodies lust. We refer, too, to a broad spectrum of psychological experience when we speak of Eros.

There's no Eros in this group. These words were spoken to me by an experienced Jungian analyst who had recently moved to New England. She meant to imply that, in comparison to her experience with other groups of analysts, our Boston meeting lacked something. I pretty well knew what she meant. There was a good deal of the "gray box world" in our meeting. We displayed little joy in our fellowship, what the Germans call *Gemütlichkeit*, a fuzzy geniality, the hearty glow of comrades who have been tramping up mountains and down valleys all day long. There was something guarded and mistrustful about us. We were reluctant to share ourselves. We showed no enthusiasm for our common work or our separate projects. We were "all business." There was no flow, no spilling over, no emotional infection from one colleague to another. We were polite, dour, and contained. No wonder attendance was low. We were a dreadful group, lacking both strife and affection. Apathy reigned.

When Eros is spoken of this way, there is no suggestion of sexual feelings. What is meant is a general interpersonal vitality. Without this kind of Eros, couples and groups are sluggish and dispirited. If we say there is a lack of passion, we imply that without it our life together as human beings is barely tolerable . In the language of the archetypal field, *Eros* is what animates our meetings and gives them soul. But the experiential realities this name evokes are very well known by everyone. Even the persona field is aware that encounters are sometimes lively and sometimes moribund. We speak of interest, affect, and involvement. We mean that we are engaged, moved, drawn in.

In this sense, every psychotherapy looks to Eros, by whatever name. But if we say *therapeutic relationships do not work unless they are erotic*, we run the risk of being misunderstood despite the universality of the truth we mean to express. As the Son of Chaos, Eros brings confusion, and as the Son of Aphrodite, lust. With our omnipresent wariness for being mistaken in such an emotionally charged dispute, we are careful about what we say.

A man who was seeing me for supervision introduced his problem with a new patient by saying, *The moment she passed through the door, the room was charged with Eros.* Clearly he did not mean merely that he felt a fellowship with this woman or that he knew they would be able to converse with interest. He meant that he felt Chaos threatening, and with unmistakable sexual overtones. Much to his relief, he found that the sexual feelings diminished substantially in succeeding weeks. But Chaos continued to threaten. He found himself alternately pulled in by a boundless neediness and cast universes away by outbursts of rage.

His account, by reason of its contrasts, made me think of a patient of mine tormented by a need to possess and worship me, combined with a terror of intimacy which kept her locked so tightly in a shell I was unable to feel her violent emotions. I had immense compassion, but the channel that might have been empathy was cut off by the casing of her fear. Although she was gray and wrinkled, I saw her as a skinny, naked girl of four or five, crouching, her chin on her knees, arms locked tightly over her shins—inside a glass cube—watching me warily out of the corner of her eye.

If Eros was in the room when I sat with that woman, it took a peculiar form. There was so little fellowship I often thought I might as well be working with an alien that had learned my language, albeit imperfectly. Yet I was bound. Although unable to return her feelings for me in kind, I could not accept an invitation to go out of town without first calculating what effect it would have on her. We might say that her obsession for me had induced a peculiar reciprocity on my side. If it was Eros that brought us together, it was certainly not at all as lovers—perhaps as father/mother/god and alien waif. I found myself in a field of fragility. The very air felt frail and brittle. I was a clumsy lout in a storeroom of delicate glasswork, an inept divinity unused to worship.

I loved that woman, though it may seem peculiar to say I loved her erotically. I am even more reluctant, however, to use the other two expressions we have inherited from the Greeks to designate love. *Philia* denotes friendly affection, and *agape* Christian charity. These terms suggest a calm centeredness that denies the chaotic passion we ascribe to *eros*. I felt myself drained, thrown into confusion, and on dangerous ground. I feared my clumsiness in that I could easily "say the wrong thing" and inflict even more pain and turmoil upon her. Indeed I did so, all too often.

My competence as a therapist was called into question, even my competence as a human being to respond to a fellow creature. The very ground of my existence was challenged by this patient, the assumptions on which I based my life, the philosophy that underlay my teaching and writing and that articulated everything I had known about myself. I felt passionately about these things. I was compelled to grapple with them and to find a way to respond to this woman simply and from my heart.

In this we were surely similar, for her passion battered and surged against the inside walls of her glass cage. Her feelings, as she sometimes named them, were even sexual in a naive, childish way. She fantasized marrying me as purely and impossibly as my friend's four-year-old daughter had done some twenty years earlier.

If we have trouble agreeing that *Eros* charged the interpersonal field between me and my severely inhibited patient, it may be the lack of symmetry that gives us pause. When we consider the analysts' meeting that *had no Eros*, surely it was symmetrical passions that we missed. Colleagues vitally engaged in their professions and their lives are expected to be able to share these things, to overflow with psychic energy and infect one another with their kindred enthusiasm. But lack of symmetry does not seem so much a problem when we consider the relationship between me and my friend's daughter. My adult affection and her childish emotionality flowed and bonded us, as she showed me her crayon drawings and somersaulted in and out of my lap while I talked with her father of politics and social justice. That little girl and I felt passionately about one another in a manner that went beyond *philia* and *agape*. Our love was erotic, although innocent of sexuality and lacking symmetry.

Symmetry, too, was evidently lacking between Dr. Mathews and his patient/lover/victim mentioned in the *Globe* article. The report implied she had sued him for sexual impropriety, unassailable evidence that his feelings for her were not reciprocated in kind. Yet this asymmetry does not at all stand in our way of agreeing that their relationship was erotic in the usual sense of the word. We often speak of love relationships being out of balance, particularly when one party does not return the other's love. We have no trouble calling these one-sided bonds erotic. Consequently we must look for some other factor if we have difficulty agreeing that my relationship with my glass-caged patient owed its power and fascination to Eros.

Possibly we hesitate on account of the unmistakable *inhibition* that characterized our sessions. Surely inhibitions played a crucial role in keeping Eros *out* of the meeting of analysts described above. Furthermore, the evidence for erotic energies in Dr. Mathews' dealings with his patient/lover/victim rests very heavily upon his *lack* of restraint—both in the fact that he allowed their relationship to become physical and in his struggle to name what it was she meant to him. Finally the uninhibited playfulness between me and my friend's little daughter supports our willingness to speak of Eros in describing the relationship.

There seem to be good reasons to build a case for the incompatibility of Eros and inhibition. But we are not consistent on this point. Presumably we would have no difficulty agreeing that Dr. Mathews

25

should have inhibited his sexual response to his patient, regardless of how erotically he was drawn to her. And when my supervisee reported that *the room was filled with Eros,* we are confident from his anxiety that he had been successful in inhibiting his response although he feared he might not be able to maintain his composure.

Clearly therefore, inhibition and erotic energies are not mutually exclusive. In fact we sometimes become alerted to the erotic nature of an interpersonal connection when inhibition emerges as a problem for us. We feel ourselves in danger of being overwhelmed by a need to express, ratify, and further the bonding impulse. Even in our private lives when unfettered by considerations of duty or conflicting commitments, we may very well be afraid of the Chaos this draw toward another may occasion in our orderly world. We hesitate and inhibit with the result that the impulse seems to gain in strength.

In a therapeutic relationship there is no question that our commitments will conflict with the erotic impulse; and in most cases we direct our attention to how, why, when, and to what extent the therapist may be expected to inhibit his response. It is hard to avoid the conclusion that inhibitions—present or absent—are almost always a problem when Eros enters the space between us.

But with regard to my glass-caged patient, we remark at the strength of *her* inhibitions. That is where the main problem seems to lie. We might be inclined to say that her passion remained locked inside of her and never overflowed to take possession of the interpersonal field. If so, was Eros barred from the therapeutic interaction? It would be hard to say so. For despite all its frustrations, her passion bound us to one another and awoke a different but equally vital set of emotions in me. This was so much the case that *our relationship itself became the primary issue between us.* Even though her inhibitions were overwhelmingly unconscious (in contrast to the predominantly conscious ones we just considered) and even though these inhibitions cut short her passion before it could flow out of her, they still determined our interaction and kept our attention on *us.*

Perhaps the most general and comprehensive thing we can say of Eros is that when he enters the room our *we-ness* takes center stage, the numinosity of our connection to one another enters our mutual consciousness. In this sense, surely, my work with the glass-caged woman was erotic. The same applies to Dr. Mathews and to my supervisee. In an attenuated way it also applies to the dull professional meeting we have considered. For insofar as we remained in our "gray boxes" that evening, we never experienced ourselves as a *we*.

In summary, it can be said that our meetings must be sufficiently erotic to bring *us* to presence, to engage us, and to make our common work interesting enough to pursue. But at higher energies the erotic factor forces our *we-ness* to the forefront and makes our relationship itself the central issue. In such situations we have no choice but to address our mutuality directly—both in terms of the *we*'s seductive power and our fear that it will dissolve our identity as an *I*.

In the foregoing discussion we have discussed Eros entering the room as though unbidden. There are times, however, when we speak in another way. We might say, possibly of a patient, that *he eroticizes all his relationships*. As far as I have been able to observe, it is primarily of *other individuals* that we say such things. This is "interpretation" talk, and we may wish to enquire as to its implications.

Evidently we mean that the alleged eroticizer finds himself in erotic relationships so frequently as to appear an exception to some unspecified norm. We imply that when he separately encounters A, B, and C—individuals who only infrequently find themselves in relationships where *we-ness* obtrudes as the central issue—we fully expect two or three of the meetings will be highly charged with erotic energy. We grant that some individuals seem to be immune to his erotic influence. But we observe *we-ness* so frequently coming to presence in his encounters that we hold him personally responsible for this state of affairs. We imply that there is an imbalance of some kind; for Eros, Son of Chaos, God of Lust, seems to enter every room when he passes through the door. We call him an "eroticizer" because his partners generally find him irresistible. *We-ness* really does obtrude chaotically again and again for him.

How does the alleged eroticizer himself experience these meetings? My exposure to such individuals leads me to conclude that generally—perhaps universally—they find themselves as much the recipients of erotic attention as do their partners. They do not voluntarily invoke Eros and may even be surprised and baffled by his frequent presence. For them as for us, Eros comes without being called, bringing the *we* inescapably to presence.

When we say *Eros generally comes unbidden* into our meetings, we are speaking of our conscious experience only. The people we call "eroticizers" are for the most part as ignorant as anyone else of how and when Eros enters the room. But the very fact that we have found and labeled such a class of individuals implies something else essential about our view of Eros and the erotic. In claiming that some individuals, whether they know it or not, have a special capacity for generating erotic energies, we imply that Eros *is* called. Not consciously perhaps, but called nevertheless. We imply an unconscious will that calls even while we remain unaware of it.

Possibly it comforts us to think that when the Son of Chaos enters the field between a couple, he may have been called by one and not by the other. Perhaps it minimizes *our* responsibility that our unconscious will has only *welcomed* the erotic confusion into which we fall. Someone else has initiated it. Responsible for its origins or not, however, we find ourselves in a difficult situation that presses for decisive action. When we ask who did it and how did it get started, we may be searching for some sort of orientation in our confusion. But whatever answers we get for these questions, we are left facing the essential issue: what are we going to do about it?

As the answer to this question will always be the individual response of a particular therapist to a particular patient met in an erotic field unique to that couple, it will not be possible to review all the possibilities. What can be done, however, is to provide a general frame for the question and its decisive response. We need a phenomenological description of the therapeutic field when Eros enters it so disruptively as to take us beyond the stage of "sufficient interest" to the point where our *we-ness* becomes a problem. We need to grasp the *structure of erotic interaction*. We shall begin by considering the nature of the erotic field as it may manifest in *any* human interaction. Thereafter we shall take up the specific peculiarities of the therapeutic situation.

Whenever Eros is felt as a disruptive force, our *we-ness* has come so forcibly to presence that our *I-ness*, our individual identity, is called into question. *I* and *you* as distinct entities are overshadowed by a numinous *we* that would subsume the qualities that define us as independent persons and dissolve us into a unity. It is the distinguishing characteristic of Eros that he lends to this *we* such a compellingly attractive force that we do not simply wonder if we can stand against it. We *want* to dissolve. Generally it seems to us that we have never wanted anything so vitally in all our lives. We view the impending unity of our *we-ness* as momentously significant. Our familiar sense of our isolated selves seems paltry in comparison. We would gladly shuck the confining limitations of our past and present self-image as a cruel delusion, now happily outgrown.

The *we*, however, does not simply fascinate us as a distant possibility. We find we are already part of it. Although dissolution lies before us as a seductive opportunity, we feel we are even now incomparably more than we were a moment ago. Enlargement, numinous *becoming*, is already underway. Paradoxically, we find we have never been so much ourselves as we are at this instant. We are in the hands of a benevolent fate, witness to a glorious revelation, transformed at the root of our being. We stand on new ground, understanding profoundly and for the first time the unity of *all* beings. Our sense of *we-ness* is the window and door upon a new life. Our eyes are opened, the world becomes animate.

The *we* comes to presence, however, only through the unique and irreplaceable *you*. It may even seem to me that you constitute our *we* more essentially even than I. For I have been "just myself" all my life, but you seem to have brought our *we-ness* with you. It was unimaginable without you and distinctively *belongs* to you. Its every precinct is redolent of *your* unique personhood. You dominate the *we* so thoroughly that I may even forget my own participation and believe that it is in *you* that I wish to dissolve. It never occurs to me and cannot be the case that you are a mere occasion for my entering this *we*. You hold my fate as no other individual could ever do. For I have no fate more momentous and compelling than that which is brought to presence in the *we* which you and I comprise.

This is the work the Greeks ascribed to Eros, the Bringer of Union. He infects us to the core of our being, transforming us into a single pole of a dyad that yearns to trade its duality for a luminous oneness in which all meaning and vitality seem to dwell. But in the midst of this immense draw, a dissent rings out. Deep in our conservative and habitual sense of being our own unique selves, we rebel against this union. We view with horror all that we have known of ourselves being lost irreplaceably.

We find ourselves on the brink of disaster, our balance deeply compromised, an instant away from plunging into the death of our individuality. All our instincts for self-preservation are mobilized and thrown into high gear. We steady ourselves against the rock of our remembered identity and prepare to flee. We shield ourselves with notions of having been deluded and blinded in our longing to dissolve. We rehearse a catalogue of our life-long beliefs and aspirations and hope they are strong enough to hold out against a demonic force that would destroy them. We step back from the precipice, and breathe deeply to calm our beating heart. But we do not turn tail; for the moment we lean away, our *we-ness* calls out to us with even greater urgency; and we prepare again to jump.

As we oscillate thus between the forward urge to dissolve and the panic to retreat, our anxiety becomes overwhelming. This is the work of Eros, Son of Chaos. Temptations to terminate the tension abound. Among the most common forms are rage, lust, and flight.

When I react with rage to the intolerable anxiety our *we-ness* generates, I hold you responsible for the pain of my fragmentation. I hardly recognize myself as the victim of this devastating urge to dissolve and equally powerful need to flee. Your appearance has confronted me with such an insuperable inner division I fear I may never be whole and intact again. I convince myself that you are personally responsible for this state of affairs.

In bringing about the loss of my coherent sense of being a self, which you alone have accomplished, I can hardly avoid the conclusion that you actually wish for my destruction. You embody all the evil forces of seduction, malice, and hatred that would bring me down, humiliate, and annihilate me. In self defense I believe I must either destroy you or erect an impenetrable wall between us. My rage is that murderous and frantic that it distorts and denies your unique personhood, replacing you with a distorted and demonic cipher that is not at all you but the projection of all my fears. In destroying you I destroy as well the *we* that emerges between us. I seek to banish Eros and return to my narrow and isolated sense of *I*, my illusory independence and self-sufficiency.

If rage radically denies erotic mutuality in an attempt to restore the *status quo ante*, lust would seem to be its polar opposite. For lust moves me to approach you as aggressively and one-sidedly as rage drives you away. But it seeks to terminate my anxiety just as resolutely. When I lust for you, I gaze upon you with eyes of desire, seeing in you all that I have failed to be myself. You are the apple of my eye. You are a revelation of numinous otherness, an embodiment of all I might become. I feel I cannot fully exist without you. I am obsessed with the need to leap the distance between us, resolve the tension that separates us and drives me crazy with desire. I need you as I have never needed anyone or anything before in my life.

I believe that if only you will give yourself to me, I will be able to possess both our *we-ness* and myself. I want to join you to myself and end the torment of my indecisive oscillation between the *me* and the *us*. I would avoid the dissolution of my identity in the seductive *we* by adding *you* onto myself as an object that enlarges but does not challenge my habitual sense of who *I* am. In so doing, I reduce your unique otherness and autonomy to a set of qualities that I may employ for my own purposes. Lust, therefore, denies the *you* while hoping to preserve the *we*. But it deludes itself in so doing, for there is no *we* without *you*. Eros, God of Lust, appears as a distortion of the Son of Chaos, a narrow and self-defeating ruler confined to the bad lands of his former domain.

Ultimately, although they move in opposite directions, lust and rage seek the same end. They want to truncate the call of Eros in order to escape Chaos and anxiety. They are modalities of flight. Rage flees the tension between the *I* and the *we* by attacking the *you* that co-constitutes the *we*. Lust flees that same tension by trying to absorb the *you* into the *I* while negating the *we*. In flight we may avoid both lust and rage by turning tail at the first sign of anxiety before we have a chance to discover our capacity for either of those dark emotions.

There is also a fourth possibility. We may take flight from the challenge posed by lust or rage themselves without ever coming to appreciate the pure call of the *we* as a distinct possibility. Finally, we may flee our *we-ness* by alternately embracing both of the other truncating emotions. In such a case our passionate erotic relationship will be characterized by outbursts of rage and lust, amounting to a dramatized and inauthentic mutual attempt to escape the tension that threatens to destroy while restoring the very same tension in its aspect of vitalizer.

The structure of erotic interaction, as it has been observed so far, makes it fairly clear that the call of Eros discernible in our *we-ness* can be heard and responded to only when the two of us can maintain both our own separate integrity and our participation in the unity that comes to presence between us. The urge to abort the tension between the *I* and the *we* may seem more than we can bear. But when I am able to bear this tension, I enable *you* to come to presence in your full and unique otherness.

Instead of attaching myself to a single limited image of you—as in lust or rage—I allow you to be yourself in all your manifold otherness. I get to know the many facets of your being and how they express your center, the nucleus of your personhood. A process of revelation takes place, as I get to know you over time and enjoy your becoming. You do the same with respect to me. We reveal ourselves to one another; and as we do so, each of us comes to discover his and her own identity anew.

In this development our *we-ness*, which we never leave, becomes a kind of lens for bringing one another and ourselves into focus. We influence one another and grow in the light of the *we* that challenges us and draws us after itself. Sexuality may be one of the many modes of our relating. But not having the one-sided and possessive character of lust, sexuality follows the call of Eros and resides in the *we-ness* that is brought to presence. If our individuality dissolves, as it surely will repeatedly, it restores itself naturally, changes, and grows.

This *structure of erotic interaction*[1] applies to all human relationships, including those conducted on the field of therapy. Considerations peculiar to therapy—such as the therapist's responsibility for maintaining boundaries of a particular kind—will emerge as refinements to this general picture. Specifically, there can hardly be any debate that a therapist is required by the nature of the profession to pay special attention to the patient's well-being and that this may involve a special kind of caution.

The Dr. Mathews, who stumbled through all the possible female relationship roles before settling on "my special lover" to describe his former patient, surely was insufficiently cautious. We may suspect him of fleeing a powerful *we*-centered pull through the tension-releasing mechanism of genital sexuality. We have no doubt that he enjoyed physical intimacies with his patient, and her raging reaction implies she felt he had gotten too close. If she had wanted their love-making to continue, she would not have sued him. Something had gone wrong between them.

There would appear to be two main possibilities—not at all mutually exclusive. If the numinous pull of the *we* had frightened her, the rage might have been generated by nothing Dr. Mathews actually did or said. Possibly she avoids all situations of intense intimacy because

[1] Described at length in Haule, 1990.

33

her sense of self is too precarious to risk obliteration in the promised unity of any *we* at all. Certainly Mathews should have known this or at least investigated the stability of her ego. If he acted in ignorance of or disregard for her uniquely personal set of fears, his behavior failed to respect her individuality. This is the second possibility. He failed to take sufficient care of her *you-ness*. Very likely he wished to possess her lustfully.

But his words do not sound like a man in the grips of Eros, God of Lust. True enough, he does speak possessively of *my* sister, wife, etc.; but he stands in awe before her. We may even detect a tone of adoration in his attitude. It reminds me very much of a passage from Teresa of Avila's *Conceptions of the Love of God*.

> But when this most wealthy Spouse desires to enrich and comfort the Bride still more, He draws her so closely to Him that she is like one who swoons from excess of pleasure and joy and seems suspended in those Divine arms and drawn near to that sacred side and to those Divine breasts. Sustained by that Divine milk with which her Spouse continually nourishes her and growing in grace so that she may be enabled to receive His comforts, she can do nothing but rejoice. . . . With what to compare this [the soul] knows not, save to the caress of a mother who so dearly loves her child and feeds and caresses it. (Pike, 1992, p. 75).

The gender and role confusions in this passage, where elements of father, husband, mother, lover, and savior are inextricably mixed, characterize many of the writings of the Christian mystics—and the documents of other religious traditions, as well. For example, the Sufis often speak of Allah as entangling the mystic in "her" dark tresses. The sephiroth of the Jewish Kaballah designate dimensions of father, mother, son, and female lover within the Godhead. Hinduism names a plethora of divinities of varying genders and roles, all as personifications of the One, *nirguna brahaman*, which is beyond all specification.

Universally, the testimony of religious mystics demonstrates how "full" the *we* may become. The fact that human lovers may slide over into mystical language complements the tendency in mystics to draw upon expressions of human sexuality. All of this adumbrates the experience of the *we* when it comes to presence with archetypal numinosity.

To say that Dr. Mathews is lying to us and to himself when he speaks of "sister, wife, mother, another friend, daughter," and "special lover," denies the phenomenological truth of his experience. No wonder he feels we are prattling about the habits of monkeys. He believes that the *we-ness* he has encountered in the presence of his patient/lover/victim has transported both of them to the "garden of pomegranates" where the "gray box" rules of the persona field are irrelevant. Appeals to ethical codes and guidelines will always seem destructive and distorting to him. If we are going to communicate with him, we need a language that does justice to the realities of both the persona field and the archetypal garden.

A phenomenological description of the structure of erotic interaction provides such a commonality of discourse. Here we can grant Dr. Mathews the mystical dimensions of the *we* as he has experienced it without relinquishing our right to speak of the interpersonal nature of that *we*—of how it presumes both the *I* and the *you*, of how it arouses a nearly unbearable tension between the tendency to dissolve in sublime unity and the tendency to maintain our coherent and habitual sense of ourselves. We can speak of his patient's rage and inquire into its purposes—whether her ego was too weak to sustain *any* numinous *we* and whether he had assumed too much about her *you*. Perhaps he will come to see that the real and transcendental experience of *we-ness* that has meant so much to him deserves a cautious respect *on its own terms* and not simply because some gray ethics code says so.

Two

Where Are Our Boundaries?

After congratulating ourselves on having slipped the shackles of Victorian prudery through the so-called sexual revolution, we now find ourselves concerned with "boundaries." While Eros dissolves what separates us and draws us into a unity, *boundaries* has become the psychological catch-word of the 1980s and 1990s. Psychological theories regarding "boundaries" have become current in a period of time when erotic feelings have been judged supremely dangerous. We say that people would not commit sexual violations, if they only "had boundaries." The "victims," too, are generally people who "have no boundaries." For the "perpetrator" to violate boundaries is a moral failing, a heedless giving way to the powerful draw of Eros.

For the victims it is a condition of weakness imposed by earlier perpetrators who habitually treated them as though personal and erotic boundaries did not exist. They have never "learned" about boundaries and therefore allow themselves to be intruded upon constantly—especially in the sexual realm. Our primary task as therapists and responsible citizens is to resist Eros and "uphold boundaries." On the one hand, we expect ourselves to be "aware of boundary issues" and to consciously "observe boundaries" and refrain from "crossing" them. When we do not have the "ego strength" to "recognize boundaries" and to keep ourselves within "appropriate boundaries," we will surely be a danger to our patients.

When we engage in ethical reflections like these, we generally apply the term *boundary* to therapists in the sense of superego expectations. We refer to our responsibility to the public world to conduct ourselves as "professionals." We perceive violations as forms of "sexual acting out," implying that sometimes our erotic impulses may escape our vigilance. Here the line between moral failure and neurosis is nearly impossible to draw. But the very fact that we see it as a matter of ethics implies that our boundary expectations for ourselves as therapists reside primarily in the conscious realm.

Our use of the term *boundaries* when we speak of our patients, however, is quite another matter. Here we refer to faulty personality structure. We describe a healthy ego as recognizing clear demarcations between self and world. Neurosis—or worse, narcissistic dysfunction—manifests in "permeable boundaries." In the most severe cases we speak of our patients as relating to others as though they were parts of themselves or as if the patients had become fused with these others.

We recognize in some of them an almost uncanny ability to zero in on the weaknesses or secrets of the people they meet—particularly their therapists. We say this is due to their almost total "lack of boundaries." "Healthy boundaries," too, are missing between their egos (their sense of having a coherent and continuous identity) and their unconscious. They are vulnerable to being overtaken by primitive emotions and ideas. Their "ego boundaries" dissolve in the face of unconscious forces. Only the most benign cases can be "taught about boundaries." The others require something far more basic: developing a sense of having a self that might someday "recognize its boundaries."

We attribute so many kinds of things to the presence or absence of "boundaries" that the term seems to know no bounds. Many of us teach our patients boundary jargon, even sometimes when their boundarilessness appears well-nigh intractable. Justification for this surely resides in our fear of Eros, whose dissolving effects are certainly unsettling and even dangerous. But the implications of our making

Eros the enemy have not been examined. We take it for granted that establishing barriers between ourselves will make us independent subjects, free of crippling dependency upon one another; and we insist upon this precisely in therapy where feelings of dependency are likely to be particularly strong. We might well wonder what effect this has on the therapeutic process.

It is by no means unusual to find therapists who understand their own psychological development entirely in terms of "boundaries." Generally they are individuals who themselves have had to learn about "boundaries" the hard way. They have come to their profession along much the same path that most drug therapists have followed, by experiencing in their own lives the destructive effects of erotic ego-dissolution. This gives them an incontrovertible authority concerning the destructive effects of Eros and allows them to present themselves as models of a new-found sobriety.

Peter Rutter presents such a case in his book, *Sex in the Forbidden Zone*. (Rutter, 1989, pp. 88-90). A psychotherapist in her early forties identified as Barbara Forsch recounts her seduction two decades earlier of a psychiatrist she calls Dr. Adams. The two of them carried on a year-long sexual relationship during their therapy sessions. With twenty years' hind-sight she has come to understand the whole episode as the crucial, definitive event in her life-long struggle to define her boundaries. Her work to understand what happened to her with Dr. Adams led her to a reinterpretation of both her childhood and her present situation as well as to her training to become a therapist in her own right.

Although not sexually abused as a child, she experienced her parents as constantly intruding on and obliterating her boundaries, an interpretation which she believes accounts for all the "sick relationships" she has had with men. At the time of her interview with Rutter, she is still angry with Dr. Adams for allowing himself to be seduced. Even when she gets close to the man she is presently living with, everything that she recalls as "gross" and disgusting with her psychiatrist comes back to her and prevents intimacy.

Barbara describes her development in three extended episodes: her parents' intrusiveness during her childhood, understood as the origin and cause of her pathology; the sexual relationship with her psychiatrist, presented as the paradigmatic instance of her self-destructive boundary crossing; and the relationship with her current boyfriend, described as the way she experiences her pathology in the present.

She says only that she has had "a lot of therapy in the ten years since I stopped seeing Dr. Adams." Apparently this is where she learned to speak the language of boundaries and trained to be a therapist herself. We are left to wonder about the nine years that intervened between the end of her affair with Dr. Adams and the beginning of the "boundary therapy," for she evidently continued seeing him over an entire decade. All three of her life's chapters have been framed in terms of "boundaries." Close examination of her use of this term will uncover a host of psychological issues and therapeutic assumptions.

The central issue is the one she is still dealing with, "trying to learn how to be intimate again in a healthier way." The symptom of her ill health is the feeling *this is gross* that she has whenever she gets close to a man. She implies that her boundaries are still not well-established, and that as she moves toward intimacy the feeling of "grossness" appears as an insuperable defense holding her back from a closeness she very much desires.

Clearly "grossness" is itself a limit that sets bounds to her freedom to participate in and enjoy a sense of *we-ness* with a man she feels drawn to. But this imposed limit is not dignified with the term *boundary*. It is treated, rather, as a symptom of boundarilessness. Therefore "having boundaries" must mean to possess the freedom to set one's own limits in a manner that is harmonious with the life one would like to lead.

"Setting boundaries" becomes the primary criterion of psychological health wherein I joyfully choose where I will go and what I will do. To be unable to set my own boundaries means to be brought up short against my will by ugly emotions I cannot control, to be painfully limited in my self-expression, to be hemmed in by fear and repugnance.

The language of boundaries, as used by Barbara Forsch, is applied exclusively to her life with other people, to her inability to negotiate the structure of erotic interaction. In the brief reference to her problematic relationship with the man she lives with, she finds herself caught between two powerful forces—one drawing her closer to him and the other driving him away. Contemplated from a certain distance, the *we* that comes forcefully to presence between Barbara and her lover seems to offer the freedom, health, and marvelous connectedness of which life has long deprived her. Seen up close, when the prospect of merging into that *we* becomes immanent, she finds herself overcome with feelings of repugnance.

Suddenly the glorious *we* has become so much a threat that the *we-ness* itself is lost—and the *you* as well. Now she says: "*This* is gross. *This* is out of the question." Everything personal has disappeared behind the *this*. She does not specify what *this* may be. We know it refers to how she experiences the prospect of union with another person. Very likely it is even more specific than that. "*This*" probably refers to the sexual act itself, the fleshliness of herself and her partner, the engorgement of their sexual organs, the grasping and fumbling at one another's bodies, the greed to be penetrated and to penetrate. All of *this* is so repugnant that she retires in a panic of disgust.

If only she could set her own boundaries, her opportunity for personal intimacy would not be obliterated by an insuperable revulsion defense that was created during her childhood years by intrusive parents and solidified by the affair with Dr. Adams. Barbara's understanding of her own psychodynamics seems to imply a theory of unconscious agency.

Consciously, she wants nothing more than to dissolve in the *we*. Unconsciously, the prospect of dissolution inspires an overwhelming terror at the impending loss of her precarious *I-ness*. Such an annihilating prospect far outweighs any bliss conjured by the *we* to deceive her conscious point of view. It turns repulsive and *gross*.

She would like the flexibility to be able to move in and out of *we-ness* according to the inclination of the moment, gliding easily about in a high-tension field between the bliss of union and the loss of self. Every human erotic interaction provides this chaotic tension, and "healthy" people can enjoy the bliss without an overwhelming horror of losing themselves. Barbara cannot. The very fact that she speaks of "boundaries" implies that she wants and expects always to have a protective barrier between herself and her lover.

We all need something to prevent the loss of our individual integrity in the dissolving threat of the *we*. But do we wish to call it a *boundary*? Does not the image of a boundary around the *I* imply that the *we* can never truly be entered? Barbara is apparently so concerned with the maintenance of her fragile sense of self, that she refuses to allow it to be loosened, interpenetrated, and even rearranged by her erotic encounter with another. Can we accept this hope for ourselves? Does it not suggest a life of tenuous and unsatisfying relationships?

Do we not find a joyful enlargement of ourselves when we share a powerful experience of *we* with someone else? Are not the rewards of dissolution our most convincing motive for engaging in erotic relationships? Barbara cannot be entirely ignorant of these facts, or she would not be "trying to learn how to be intimate again in a healthier way." Because "healthy intimacy" allows for degrees of dissolution, the image of a "boundary" may be at odds with what is sought.

Although "boundaries" may provide a poor metaphor to describe the essential nature of intimacy, perhaps we can retain the concept of "ego boundaries" as an essential *stepping stone* to psychic health for one who is as "wounded" as Barbara. Possibly a "boundariless" person needs barriers between herself and others as an intermediate stage before dispensing with them in order to enjoy partial dissolution in a healthy sense of *we-ness*. Let us investigate this alternative in connection with the paradigmatic instance of Barbara's boundary crossing, the affair with Dr. Adams. What kind of intermediate stage might have been achieved?

The seduction occurred in her third meeting with him. She summarizes the earlier sessions in two sentences: *He looked real good to me by contrast with my family. I could see he was attracted to me, and I wanted to make myself important to him.* The middle-aged Barbara recalls this twenty-year-old scene as an encounter with something truly novel and even revelatory in the *we* that came to presence between herself and her psychiatrist, making him look "real good." Although she fails to elaborate what this *good* might have meant to her, we know (a) that she has never seen it before, (b) that it is so momentously significant she cannot allow it to slip out of her life, and (c) that it gives Dr. Adams the power to bestow upon her his highly valued recognition that she is "important."

We can understand Barbara's state of mind during her first two sessions of therapy quite well without resorting to boundary language. But as soon as we get to the third hour of therapy, when the seduction occurred, boundaries are everywhere. Rutter introduces Barbara's account of her seduction with an assertion about boundaries: "Women who have such unformed boundaries are at great risk to offer themselves sexually to men." He brings us up short. We are not allowed to read the account of the seduction without theoretical prompting. We are to be on the lookout for "boundaries" being violated. The seduction is then told in four sentences:

> I went to my third session with Dr. Adams with my raincoat on and nothing but underwear underneath. When it was time to go I took off my coat and rubbed up against him. He was kind of passive about it, but I could tell that he was going to let it keep happening. It just escalated from there.

The assertion that Barbara's "boundaries" are "unformed" can hardly be meant to imply that she did not recognize the presence of a social-consensus barrier. Everyone agrees that showing up for your therapy appointment in your underwear is a strikingly unconventional thing to do. Barbara had to know she was crossing a very naughty boundary. Indeed, we can hardly resist imagining her state of mind as she sat in her trenchcoat, trembling in every cell of her being with the secret of her nakedness.

She says of her disrobing, that she "sexualized" the therapy. But that is not quite accurate. The interactive field between herself and Dr. Adams had to have been charged with sexual energy the moment she entered the door with her dangerous and tantalizing but silent proposition. Perhaps she was not sure she would actually remove the coat, or at what moment during the hour. No doubt every nuance of the dialogue was scrutinized for its relevance to her probable unveiling. "Would he say that to me if he knew I was in my underwear?" "Does he suspect what my comment *really* means?"

Because the knowledge that she was crossing over into Rutter's "forbidden zone" was essential to her drama, we must conclude that her "unformed boundaries" refer to some other kind of barrier than that of social mores. She had to have known, factually, that the social and ethical boundary was implied, but it may well have been the case that she lacked a healthy fear of such dangerous crossings. The careful staging of her surprise implies she knew it was risky, but perhaps not risky enough to evoke the *gross*.

Her "sexualizing" behavior suggests that, consciously, she was impatient to *dissolve* boundaries. In this respect she was not in need of barriers but desperate to escape their confinement and isolation. Union with Dr. Adams had to have been irresistibly inviting. For, contemplated from a safe distance, dissolution in a numinous *we* always seems to promise enlargement and togetherness. Because her fear of losing herself must have been almost wholly unconscious, her drive for joining with a powerful other had to have preoccupied her as an obsessive concern.

She was convinced some kind of barrier had to be broken through—perhaps that of social expectation. "Sexualizing" served this need by stoking up the fires of the tantalizing *we*, heightening its attractiveness, recasting it as an exciting reality rather than a vague promise—the solution to her twenty-year-long agony of isolation and disconnectedness. Breaching sexual boundaries must therefore have seemed to raise the salvific power of the *we* and place it within reach.

If at the time of her third therapy session Barbara "needed bound-aries," this theoretical fact was lost on her. She was instead prepared to obliterate any barrier she could find and end her isolation. In this context, it seems paradoxical to describe her as a "woman with un-formed boundaries." For this phrase causes us to reverse our attention, directing it away from the limitations of social mores to the negligi-bility of Barbara's sense of herself.

To have an "unformed boundary" must be like having an unfrozen ice cube. The water is there all right, but cannot be gathered. It runs out between our fingers and escapes. In this way Barbara's identity is unformed and unreliable, her sense of being a self illusory and eva-nescent. She needed "boundaries" to give herself shape and definition. Evidently the *we* she contemplates between herself and Dr. Adams appears as a remedy for her boundless fluidity.

She herself has little to bring to the *we*—its definition and promise owing everything to her psychiatrist's contribution. This must so much have been the case, that it hardly deserves to be called a *we* at all. A *we* so thoroughly dominated and defined by the *you* can only be *mine* to the extent that I may be allowed to take up residence in it as a kind of unworthy guest who has no means to help with the rent. I rely upon the generosity of the *you* to give me everything I lack. Having no right to be here, I am completely dependent and hand over even my illusory identity to the *you*. In this way Barbara seeks to lose her miserable self in Dr. Adams' greater being.

If we are in search of a set of boundaries that can function as a "stepping stone" to achieving an ego capable of intimacy, we may have found it implied in Barbara's "lack of form," her undefined sense of who she is. Implicitly preoccupied with her "lack of boundaries," Barbara's life is characterized by an urgent search for a boundedness that will give shape and meaning to her life. Her "sexualizing" seems to home in on the *we* she shares with Dr. Adams, as though she has finally found the vessel into which to pour her fugitive fluidity. This would seem to be the reason "women with unformed boundaries" are said to be "at great risk to offer themselves sexually to men."[1]

[1] We might suspect the same would be true of men with "unformed boundaries" when-ever they find themselves in the presence of a *we* bearing the secure form of a more well-developed *you*.

A vessel certainly has "boundaries" that provide containment, although they are not where we expected to find them. Barbara's boundary language led us to expect to find some kind of "stepping stone" *between* herself and the others. If Dr. Adams' personality can give Barbara some sense of form intermediate to discovering herself, these are boundaries that do not separate but include. Still they may constitute the "stepping stone" we seek, very much in keeping with our ice-cube metaphor.

The boundaries of an ice cube are entirely external. Water has to be poured into a form that has nothing to do with the intrinsic structure of the liquid itself, and the form can be removed only when the water has rigidified in its externally imposed shape. As a model for finding personality structure, this metaphor agrees fairly well with Barbara's fantasy of pouring herself into Dr. Adams' vessel. But it hardly suggests a viable way of life.

A satisfying personal life implies finding some sort of "internal" form—perhaps like the virtual crystalline structure of a salt dissolved in water. In this image, the structure of my *I* remains as an invisible but indestructible reality even when I am dissolved in a numinous *we*. When I withdraw from the *we* to continue with the day-to-day necessities of life, my intrinsic shape returns—as when the water of a solution evaporates and the crystal with its characteristic structure reforms at the bottom of the beaker. According to this metaphor, to say that Barbara has "unformed boundaries" is to imply that her personal form is thoroughly "virtual" and has not yet been discovered. Again the image of a "boundary" is misleading, for it suggests something external and extrinsic whereas what is sought is a form that is internal and intrinsic.

If to "have well-formed boundaries" means to have a flexible, resilient, and reliable sense of self, it describes a significant achievement in personality development that enables a person to engage in "healthy relationships." Barbara's desire to pour her fluid and unformed self into the vessel of Dr. Adams is very far from this. But perhaps it may still be a "stepping stone."

Something of an intermediate accomplishment of this sort may be suggested in Barbara's having "considered it a triumph" to have drawn Dr. Adams into an affair. It is perhaps dangerous to think so, for it is generally agreed that the "sexualizing" of therapy is always and in every sense destructive. Barbara's "boundary therapy," in fact, takes it as a symptom of the severity of her "woundedness" that she resorted to "sexualizing." However, it may just as well have been a symptom of emerging health if there is any possibility that the affair with Dr. Adams *did* provide her a temporary sense of having a form. Could it be that the seduction accomplished something positive?

We can easily imagine how this "triumph" must have been experienced. In her third therapy session, while she sat as demurely as she was able, trembling with the salacious secret of her imminent nudity, Barbara must have been supremely aware of her power to change the whole tenor and playing field of the interaction. Loosening only three or four buttons would fracture the boundary between his agenda and hers, between therapy and sex. Only she knew the stakes of this game for sure. Locked in his innocent professional persona, Dr. Adams had become the mouse and Barbara the cat. What a change this must have been in comparison with the first two sessions, when she had been the helpless one and he the powerful healer.

In the relatively milder erotic field of the first two sessions, the *we* that came to presence between them had been dominated by the security of Dr. Adams' *you*, against which Barbara's evanescent sense of *I* must have appeared pitiful and even shamefully inadequate. In danger of being overwhelmed and rendered negligible by his powerful dominance of the *we*, she reached for what must have seemed the only weapon she had to equalize an otherwise hopelessly unbalanced relationship. If she could draw him across the sexual barrier, she would gain control of the *we*. By "sexualizing" her meeting with him, she brought about a "triumph" over a momentously significant *you*.

The results, however, are anything but clear. We know only (a) that she succeeded in converting the relationship into a year-long affair, (b) that some kind of professional association was resumed for another nine years once an agreement had been reached to end the lovemaking, and (c) that the reaction *this is gross* had its origins some time during these ten years.

Evidently the sexual relationship satisfied her for a time, if only partially. Possibly she "triumphed" over him session after session, enhancing her sense of being an *I* while retaining her perception of Dr. Adams as a marvelously powerful *you*. At some point this state of affairs ended, and the "triumph" was rendered impossible by the emergence the *gross*. Even if some form of the *gross* had been implicitly present in the first sexual encounter, a full year had to pass before insuperable revulsion could establish itself as an effective barrier against continuing the sexual interaction.

This would be true even if Barbara had not been the one to terminate the affair. Perhaps Dr. Adams ended the lovemaking at the end of a year in such a way as to imply to Barbara that her "sexualizing" was "gross." All we know for sure is that sexual intimacy had become repulsive to her, although her psychiatrist continued to "look good" enough for her to go on seeing him for another nine years.

It would not be unreasonable to suppose that an imbalance persisted in the *we*. Although Dr. Adams was made a trifle more human by his fall, he must have remained so marvelously powerful that Barbara continued to feel more "important" by spilling her runny *I* into the vessel of his *you*, week after week for a full decade. During this time her ego must have gradually firmed up to the point that her sense of being an *I* became strong enough to terminate their association. Such a development implies that termination had to have been a greater victory than seduction. Nevertheless, she found herself in pretty bad shape after saying good-bye to Dr. Adams. She could no longer avoid the conclusion that her "triumph" had been illusory in that it had confirmed only the "grossness" of her attempts at sexual intimacy.

While sexual dissolution had become "gross" and a symptom of her lack of conscious self-determination, her anger at Dr. Adams' compliance implied a growing sense of herself. At the end of the ten years, she appreciated the value of social boundaries for the first time— through the deep injury to her selfhood that came to presence as "grossness." In this sense the *gross* is a manifestation of emerging health. Formerly she was without any sense of personal shape and desperately in search of external bounds to contain herself. Now she knows that some forms of containment are counterproductive and "gross." The *gross* has emerged unconsciously as a defense against continuing to rely on the "stepping stone" of extrinsic boundaries inappropriate to her nascent sense of intrinsic form.

Implicitly healthy though the emergence of the *gross* may have been in marking Barbara's progress from "sexualizing" to rage, its persistence over a period of a full decade represents the failure of Barbara's therapeutic work with Dr. Adams. Although she may underestimate what her psychiatrist has done for her, she is fully justified in resenting his failure. This, too, is understood in terms of the "boundaries" *he* failed to observe and maintain. He cooperated with her impulse to violate the barrier of social mores, and in an indecisive and inauthentic manner: *He was kind of passive about it, but I could tell that he was going to let it keep happening. It just escalated from there.*

Barbara's account makes it unmistakable that her psychiatrist was presented with a temptation he had not the integrity to resist. He doubtless knew he was crossing a forbidden boundary and assumed the role of a coy maiden seduced against his better judgment but willing to go ahead as long as it is clear that she is the initiator. If we say he "had no boundaries" we surely do not mean he was unaware of violating an ethical barrier. If he failed to appreciate the psychological enormity of his act as regards his patient's well-being, his relation to sexuality (his own and human sexuality, generally) must have been quite unconscious. If he was blinded by his own uncontrollable needs, the intrinsic structure of his own self must have been "unformed" in some essential manner.

It is easy to imagine how he experienced his third session with her. He had to have been aware in the first two meetings that the erotic energy between them was a significant factor. Very likely he had already found Barbara and the prospect of working with her for an extended period especially interesting. When she arrived for her third session bubbling over with her secret proposal, he had to have felt a huge increase in the erotic charge. Her remarks, gestures, and glances as the hour progressed had to have been very arousing. Her boundlessness must have been intensely exciting; and her search for a vessel into which to pour herself must have appealed both to his fatherly and to his sexual feelings, inflating him in his own eyes and making him believe that he was uniquely suited to draw her into himself and "heal" her.

In this way Barbara's "wound" called out loud and clear through its "sexualizing" of the atmosphere and found an answer in her psychiatrist's "wound." Evidently he needed her dependency as badly as she needed his receptivity. As the *we* became more and more compelling and mysterious through the heightening of erotic tension, both people must have been fascinated. At the moment of her disrobing, however, the *we* vanished behind her nakedness as the wanton gift she felt compelled to give and the tantalizing possession he longed to make his own. Only the passivity of his temporary pose remained as a flimsy obstacle to the lust that would collapse the last vestiges of the *we* into *mine* and *yours*.

If Dr. Adams had received the fugitive liquidity of her sexual self and valued it in such a way as to make her feel "important" (i.e., a valued and unique individual), she would have found herself empowered and not merely "triumphant." Something essential went awry, and the middle-aged Barbara has identified it: *He could have said, "I see what you're doing, and I totally understand, but I can't do this with you. Let's talk about what goes on inside you that you have to do this."*

To "understand" a person's behavior means to *see* it for what it is within the full context of her individuality—grasped as a whole and in its "parts." Thus, Barbara wanted both to be *seen* and to learn to *see* herself. Although unaware of this double need at the time of her third therapy session, she embodied it with her nudity. In accepting her sexual agenda, Dr. Adams complied with the embodiment but failed to raise it to the level of *seeing* and "understanding."

Sex was brought into an on-going interactive field as a crude and inarticulate statement having at least three unconscious meanings for Barbara: (a) can you see *me* and not just my "parts"; (b) if there is anything valuable about me, can you hold it securely and help *me* to see what it is; or (c) will you let me manipulate you like a "naughty boy," proving that everything powerful about me is "gross"? Although Barbara was left to carry the burden of *grossness* as the most obvious outcome of her ten year association with Dr. Adams, we have seen that some progress (albeit insufficient) was made in her coming to appreciate her own sense of selfhood. The best evidence of this is the rage that enabled her to terminate the therapy.

Again boundary language has provided only the most superficial appreciation of the dynamics of the interpersonal field between a therapist and a badly "wounded" patient. But perhaps there remains one area where it may still contribute something essential: Barbara's account of the origins of her "woundedness." *Woundedness*, in boundary language, is used interchangeably with "having inadequate boundaries." Rutter tells the story of Barbara Forsch, in fact, to illustrate one of "the wounds of women." A "wound" is an injury sustained by an organism that was once "whole"; and it can be "healed" with appropriate treatment.

Barbara sees herself as having been born whole but wounded by the "boundary invasions" of her parents. Not having experienced any other way of being, she had not *known* she was "wounded" when she began seeing Dr. Adams. Instead she *enacted* her "woundedness" with him, exploring its failures, triumphs, and "grossness" with vivid clarity— but without coming to identify it as "wounded behavior" for at least a decade. In this way her ten years with Dr. Adams came to constitute a detailed case study of her profoundly injured personality and an object of close scrutiny. In her "boundary therapy," it became her model for appreciating both her current difficulties in intimate relationships and her childhood.

To have such a well-known and deeply analyzed paradigm to study offers immeasurable benefits to the process of self-understanding. But it is clear from Barbara's account that once she had identified her psychological condition as "wounded," the focus of her therapy drifted away from the paradigm itself and back to the putative origins of her injury. Her childhood experience became explanatory—both of the boundarilessness she manifested in her affair with Dr. Adams and in her present difficulties with intimacy.

She believes her parent's invasions *started literally the day I was born* through their criticism and organizing of her spontaneous play. We can take this to mean that she wonders if she was ever "whole" and has to consign her pre-wounded state to the unconscious past of earliest infancy. Her remembered history is all of a piece, culminating in the boundary violations with Dr. Adams, albeit somewhat ameliorated by her recent ten years of therapy.

She is more explicit about how her development of a dependable sense of "boundaries" was frustrated during her teenage years. Her mother repeatedly warned her about boys and suspected her of sexual misconduct, refusing to believe Barbara's honest protestations to the contrary and ignoring her requests for "real information" about sex. *She went through my drawers, opened my mail, listened in on phone calls, and checked my underpants when I took them off—anything that had to do with me was for my mother's hands and eyes.*

These are apparently the facts she knew and resented as a teenager. However, the middle-aged Barbara provides two more comments that reveal the interpretation these facts have been given in her "boundary therapy." *I felt parts of my body belonged to other people. Because my boundaries were so messed up, it was almost inevitable that I would not be the one to perceive that I shouldn't have sex with my shrink.*

We have already addressed the second of these claims and reached two conclusions: (a) that she could not have been ignorant of the social consensus that frowns on having "sex with her shrink" although she evidently failed to appreciate the wisdom of this "boundary" and (b) that the "lack of boundaries" driving her into "sexualizing" the therapy had much more to do with the negligibility of her sense of having an *I* and a relentless quest to find a form to hold her fluidity.

Her teenage memories clearly support these earlier conclusions. The maternal harangues made it clear at least that pre-marital sex was forbidden—of which "sex with her shrink" would surely be an instance. Furthermore, her mother's invasiveness rendered Barbara an object devoid of personal integrity. We have no trouble at all accepting Barbara's middle-aged interpretation that the groundwork of her impoverished sense of herself was laid by the mistreatment she suffered in her childhood environment.

But now she adds a claim we have not considered: *I felt parts of my body belonged to other people.* Following immediately after the details of her mother's intrusions into her private life, this statement introduces her interpretation that she was incapable of seeing "sex with her shrink" as inadvisable. The sequence of sentences is evidently designed to convince us that because her letters and underwear seemed to belong to her mother she thought it only natural to hand over her mouth, breasts, clitoris, and vagina to her therapist. But we resist this conclusion even though we suspect there may be a good deal of truth in it. She *protested* her mother's interest but *offered* herself to her "shrink." Furthermore, her mother did not ask for her body parts, but only what was closest to them. We need a rationale to help us grasp the difference in these two attitudes.

Perhaps she was dying for a "good mother" to whom she could hand over all her secrets and herself as well, someone who would not take her "parts" and use them against her, annihilating the *I* she barely suspected she had. *He looked real good to me by contrast with my family,* no doubt because Dr. Adams seemed to be concerned with Barbara herself, giving her hope that she might finally be an *I* and embodying the first genuine *you* she had ever encountered. A *we* came to presence for the first time in her life.

The mother who "messed up her boundaries" was therefore the first "sexualizer" in her life. She treated Barbara's private parts and possessions as impersonal sources of evidence that her daughter might be the loose woman of her own obsessions, and teaching Barbara that "cutting loose," had to be the most wonderful of forbidden fantasies. Whatever was private and redolent of sexuality possessed inestimable value and required above all to be handed over to a man who would value its "importance." A woman or girl carried her privates like liquid gold, brimming a cumbersome saucer, constantly in danger of a tragic spill. "Boys," in their insensitive greed, would upset the precarious plate and dissipate the numinous secret of her undiscovered self. It had to be handed over in order to be found. The "good mother"—or perhaps the anti-mother—would be a man who was secure, sensitive, and wise, who possessed a capacious vessel into which she could safely pour the burden of her mysterious sexual self, someone who would at last treasure it and reveal its value to her.

But to conceive this vessel as a "set of boundaries" to contain Barbara's "body parts" as her own language suggests, evokes the image of a coffin—or perhaps Isis' boat on the Nile, heaped with the limbs, trunk, and head of Osiris, as the goddess searches in vain for his missing phallus. Would it not be more appropriate to speak rather of the thread that strings together the separate beads of a necklace or the limbs of a child's "Jumping Jack"? True, enough, her mother has violated the unbounded space of her individuality to render Barbara a collection of unattached "parts." But to speak of a "boundary" to prevent the helter-skelter loss of those "parts" hardly addresses the central issue: their need for cohesion and articulation as the elements of a unified personality.

Our phenomenological description of Barbara's struggles has enabled us to understand what it means to have a "wound" characterized by "unformed boundaries" that drives a woman despite all apparent common sense ethics to "sexualize" the interpersonal field she shares with her therapist. We grasp as well why her experience of the *gross* is linked so firmly to Dr. Adams—even though her mother's salacious interest in her secrets fragmented the teenaged Barbara into a loose connection of "body parts," every one an occasion for sullying misconduct.

The "boundary-messing" family of origin spawned the notion of the *gross*, but it was enacted and experienced for the first time only with Dr. Adams. In discovering all this, however, we have had to abandon or modify essentially, every meaning she ascribes to "boundaries." Because "boundary language" obscures the issues, we are left to wonder whether Barbara's ten years of therapy since her termination with Dr. Adams may not have served her better if it had eschewed the "boundary" metaphor and sought to find a new language more immediately appropriate to her actual experience.

The boundary metaphor, in fact, appears to be a way of limiting an erotic encounter and making it safe. Its imagery demonizes Eros in its unitive moment (the pull toward dissolution and unity) and absolutizes the distancing moment in erotic tension (the tendency to resist dissolution in order to recover or to find for the first time a sense of personal identity). As such, it justifies rage and flight while seeming to make the erotic encounter safer by rejecting lust. Our analysis of boundary language makes clear how vital it is to have a more adequate understanding of Eros, and particularly to begin with a sympathetic investigation of the undervalued unitive moment in an erotic encounter.

Three

Eros and Union

When the issue of "sexualized therapy" comes up, we tend to freeze. Our language gets fuzzy. We speak in generalities as though we might be led into loosening our hold on the hottest of ethical guidelines. We are "fundamentalists" on the question of sex in connection with therapy. Cooperation by a therapist in the "sexualizing" of the work is so absolutely wrong that we cannot afford to give the impression of condoning any aspect of it. We do not wish to hear of the "niceties" of a therapist's dilemma when a therapeutic field has been "sexualized," for they sound too much like excuses. When a patient speaks as fuzzily but absolutely as this about a spouse or series of unfortunate lovers, we have no hesitation in suspecting some "complex" must be at work. We understand that when the "superego" or "persona" inspires neurotic anxiety and thereby forbids a dispassionate look at "shadow issues," we have to find a way to open them up.

It is not only therapists who have this problem. The fuzziness of the English language itself gets in the way of our attempts at developing helpful distinctions in the realm of erotic experience. For example, I would like to argue that "the erotic" refers to the energy of an interpersonal field when a sense of *we-ness* comes forcefully to presence and that "the sexual" involves an impulse to embody that *we-ness* in a genital manner. In this sense "the sexual" would be a smaller set of possibilities overlapping a more comprehensive "erotic field." Such a distinction gives us the freedom to investigate whether some situations might be "erotic" but not "sexual" and vice-versa. As useful as it might be, however, these definitions ask us to overlook the fact that the words *erotic* and *sexual* are used interchangeably in everyday speech.

For example, the text of an advertisement for telephone sex in a local newspaper reads: *Hot, horny, sex starved nympho craving raw, nasty sex.* There can be little doubt that the average reader would call this an "erotic" invitation even though there will surely be no possibility for a *we* to emerge between the caller and the self-described "nympho." It is an ad for assisted masturbation in which the paid partner is expected to play a "hot and horny" role regardless of her boredom.

The caller will encounter neither a *you* nor a *we*. Indeed, he will expect the woman to fulfill his own private fantasies; and she will cling to them, too, as a way of earning her fee and hiding herself. He will care as little about her as a personality as she will about him. Both parties will misrepresent themselves in order to generate an impersonal drama to assist the caller's achieving an orgasm. According to the distinction I would like to employ, this telephone exchange will be thoroughly "sexual" and not the least bit "erotic."[1]

Another area of potential confusion arises when a therapeutic interaction has been "sexualized"; for what appears to be a demand for sexual compliance may very well be masking some rather different and more "generally erotic" dynamic. Sometimes a sexual tension thick enough to be cut with a knife that persists for weeks or months can dissolve in a single moment, as though it had been waiting for the right question to be asked.

For example, a female colleague once described a patient who had been demanding sexual contact for weeks. The therapist was at her wits' end until it occurred to her one day to risk the appearance of compliance and ask her twenty-year-old patient exactly *how* she would like to be touched. Immediately the atmosphere changed, as the answer came back that she wanted to be held and rocked.

[1] Yet even telephone sex need not be completely one-sided, as Nicholson Baker illustrates in his novel, *Vox* (1992). The entire 164 pages are an excerpt from a telephone call between a couple who start out as strangers but come to know a good deal about one another.

At other times the tension may give rise to a clarifying image from the unconscious, as happened with a patient of mine who dreamed of being a fetus, curled up and asleep on my lap. Another woman, after day-dreaming for months of developing a romantic relationship with her analyst, finally sculpted him as a monumental sun-god, his wiry hair studded with *I Ching* coins, a kind of Aztec representation of the Tao.

When such parental or godlike images emerge from the tension, we know that "the erotic" is a much larger category than "the sexual." If we cling to a sexual understanding of our erotic feelings, it may be that the lure of sexual adventure seems a lot safer than the prospect of regressing to a fetal stage or tangling with a god. "The erotic" may, indeed, manifest as a roaring chasm of dangerous emotion in which longing for entanglement mixes with regret, desolation, despair, anger, and a terror of losing ourselves.

Whatever attracts us strongly enough to be felt through all that drives us away, will surely be felt as "erotic" and runs the danger of being interpreted as "sexual." For once we have become sexually active—and probably well before—overwhelming, primitive bonding emotions take on a sexual tone, with its nearly irresistible invitation to demolish invisible barriers. As a yearning to merge opens the center of our being in an almost bodily way, feelings associated with genital arousal occupy the center of our attention; and we become powerfully aware of our incompleteness as individuals. We think we are sexually attracted.

As a gloss on "the erotic," sexual attraction seems to tell us what to do about the chaos that strives within us. If only we can hold our partner in our arms, shed the clothing that separates us, and unite in throbbing ecstasy, all will end in peace and contentment. But alas, the more insistent the erotic tension, the more objections present themselves.

What if he's only "using" me? Where are my "values"? Does this make me a "philanderer," a "bigamist," an "immoralist"? "What kind of woman" *is* she, that she would agree to this? Where are my "boundaries"; where are his? Will I get AIDS? Will I become "addicted" to sex? I am not the person I thought I was. Are we "abusing" one another? If I do this, will I finally be rid of my "sexual hang-ups"? Am I really "glamorous and attractive" after all? A "real man" wouldn't hesitate before such an opportunity. All the articles we have perused in the check-out lines of supermarkets come back to haunt us with anticipations and doubts. Perhaps what seems so monumental is nothing but a foolish episode from a "soap opera."

Clearly erotic involvements do not occur in a vacuum. As a society we find them fascinating and dangerous. Our songs, literature, and movies are filled with the promise and misery of romantic adventures. Our laws and maxims are clear on the desirability of heterosexual monogamy and "family values," but we support a thriving and rather tawdry "pornography" industry. Despite dissent from several directions, our children are still taught that women should be soft and innocent while men are driven by a lust for sexual conquest.

At the same time, there are countless books and workshops on the transformative delights of orgasm and the techniques to achieve them. Advertising implies that sexual attractiveness is only a purchase away, providing we have the right kind of body shape. Both inhibitions and indulgence are forbidden. Lately we have become obsessed with incest and childhood sexual abuse, producing a burgeoning literature of tracts and analyses on both sides of the issue. Psychotherapies of all kinds are right in the middle: praised for uncovering it, vilified for creating it, and suspected of perpetuating it.

Inside or outside of therapy, when we find ourselves in a relationship charged with erotic energies, we bring all these societal perspectives along with us. They exert a tremendous pressure to conform ourselves with what "everybody knows" and expects. We want to acquit ourselves well and live up to a self-image that has been influenced and shaped by the world around us. Erotic experience challenges our private sense of ourselves so that we wonder if we are up to the performance standards of our society.

Are we sufficiently free of inhibition and yet not "out of control"? Are we capable of an adequate response, or will we disappoint our partner and prove ourselves an emotional cripple? Will the erotic alliance "fit in" with social expectations and merit an acceptable label (marriage, friendship, collegiality, neighborliness, mentorship) or will it lead us outside of well-worn and respectable paths and call our "normality" into question?

These are the pressures of the "persona field," the world of social roles and expectations, with its well-advertised but largely unconscious and frequently contradictory ideals and taboos. In its overwhelming concern for social conformity, the persona field would set limits to interpersonal erotic concerns. Meanwhile the *we* that Eros brings to presence calls out only to the *I* and the *you*, introducing a compelling fascination that separates the *us* from the *them*.

The *we* emerges always in a sacred space, a *temenos*,[2] separated by an invisible wall from the realm of profane social interactions going on around it. This erotic *temenos* is further characterized by the special quality of emotions inspired by the *we*. We find ourselves drawn to one another in a fateful and mysterious way, feeling that we can ignore our mutuality only at our own peril. An opportunity we can hardly afford to ignore provides us the prospect of renewal, enlargement, and self-discovery—so compellingly that the commonplace assumptions of the persona field are rendered banal and irrelevant. No wonder self-appointed spokespersons of the persona field are quick to sound the alarm and supply labels: "sexualizing," "boundary violations," "abusive," "codependent," "neurotic."

The couple inside the *temenos* is rarely immune to such an excited clamor of accusations. Indeed, they may contribute their own anxious concerns gathered from the same public supply: "where is this relationship going"; "have we lost our wits"; "what will people think?"

---

[2] *Temenos*: a sacred precinct, especially of a temple; from *temno* (Greek), meaning to cut or draw a line. Before a Greek temple was built, a single furrow was drawn at the edge of the future temple precinct to separate the sacred ground inside the line from the profane ground outside.

It requires a good deal of madness—in the best[3] or worst sense of the term—to resist the pressure of the persona field and respond to the call of the *we*. If we have the courage or intemperance to do so, an entire world of experience is opened up to us, a world whose realities are barely understood and mostly maligned by the public world of social consensus, but a world so compelling and transformative[4] that those who return from it frequently find themselves alien sojourners in the persona field.

The erotic *we* comes to presence not only between sexual lovers but anytime the relationship itself leaps to the forefront of our mutual concern. The *we* retires to the background when child and mother squabble over whether he must eat his spinach. But the moment he skins his knee and raises his hands in a wordless request to be lifted and held, the *we* has returned.

The pain and blood on his knee have brought home to him how vulnerable, alone, and frightfully mortal he is without her. His heart jumps right out of his chest in a longing arc to cling to her. He can already feel the warm press of her body as a cool, yearning hollow. Their imminent union hovers in the air between their bodies as a barely differentiated *we*, promising absolute peace and security. His mother, too, has had a passing image of losing him and a panic to wrap him in her arms. They want to dissolve into a numinous symbiosis, and they feel the thrill of drawing closer no less poignantly than a pair of lovers in an airport.

Eros can enter nearly any interpersonal field. The *we* may go unnoticed as student and professor attend to the problems of her dissertation. But when their enjoyment of one another's presence enhances the work, they have entered an erotic *temenos* even if sexual fantasies never enter their minds. Many a therapeutic relationship is filled with the luminosity of Eros without having to suffer the chaos engendered by sexual feelings.

[3] In the *Phaedrus*, Socrates says that the irrationality of love is really a kind of "divine madness" whereby we remember the eternal Forms that are revealed to the soul before she "loses her wings" and becomes incarnate.
[4] The description of this world is the subject matter of my book, *Divine Madness: Archetypes of Romantic Love* (Shambhala, 1990).

Therapist and patient may delight in one another's company and savor what they learn of each other's personality. The *we* comes to presence as the quiet, secure place where the habitual shape of their *I* softens and becomes receptive to the *you*. They follow trails of mutual interest, alive to whiffs of mysterious promise. The erotic field between them encourages sponteneity and originality. They feel they accomplish a great deal of therapeutic work every hour, possibly because every nuance of their dialogue touches them so deeply. Their *we-ness* is defined by this enriching entanglement.

The central and defining element in every erotic encounter is the coming to presence of a numinous *we* that transforms us as individuals in our experience of ourselves. Before the powerful emergence of the *we*, the two of us are separate entities engaged in a contractual enterprise as therapist and client, teacher and student, roommates, etc. But the moment Eros enters the field between us, our personalities become mutually implicated in the third, unitary principle we call the *we*. Now *I* and *you* take on a new meaning as entangled constituents of a larger *one*.

Just as the *we* cannot exist apart from my unique *I* and your unique *you*, so *I* and *you* now have a new "lived meaning" as belonging to and participating in our *us*. My experience of myself is expanded and offered new possibilities. From the very first moment I experience the *we* as "mine" as well as "ours" and feel it as a "call" to further exploration. A momentous future lurks in the *we*, awaiting realization through our cooperative activity. For, although we are already living *in* our mutuality, we are doing so only partially.

Despite our unity, we are still strangely separate; despite our separateness we are nevertheless strangely one. The *we* commands a mysterious fascination. Because my sense of myself has already been wondrously enlarged and rearranged in the erotic field I share with you, I cannot ignore the possibility that even more might be achieved if only we can find a way to dissolve our residual separateness in a more complete unity.

So natural and yet extraordinary is our encounter with mutuality, that we can hardly avoid entertaining the thought that our meeting has been predestined by "fate." This marvelous "fit" of the *I* and the *you* into our *we* seems to offer proof that we "belong" together. It is as though we have been unconsciously in search of one another all our lives. Now for the first time we have found the missing key and feel that we are on our own proper course. We reflect on our past and wonder how we could have understood ourselves so narrowly. A great deal seems to have been accomplished by the simple fact of the *we's* emergence. Not least significant is the new horizon it seems to open for us: the possibilities of mutual self-discovery through our pregnant unity.

Lovers imagine spending their lives together. Therapist and patient, although not immune to this fantasy, are bound to find their work uniquely compelling. The patient finds himself *connected* with another in a way he had not dreamed possible. Perhaps not since his infantile fusion with his mother has he felt so much a part of someone else. Even more significantly, if he experienced his parents as distant and unavailable, the relationship with his therapist becomes the fulfillment of a wish he barely knew he had. He feels "understood" as never before and begins to understand himself.

The *we* that comes to presence between himself and his therapist offers a wholeness, a containment, and a future so foreign to his impoverished past that the world outside the therapeutic *temenos* fades into shadowy insubstantiality. He can already sense what it means to be "healed" of his life-long insufficiency.

Similarly, his therapist finds herself awakened to new life. This particular patient stands out as uniquely suitable for therapeutic work, their interactions characterized by a marvelous vitality. She finds herself "coming into her own" as a therapist more fully than ever before. This is the patient curiously designed to unlock her potential and discover the fullness of her talents. She cannot become what she is without him, any more than he can thrive without her.

The agenda for every erotic interchange, therapeutic or otherwise, resides in the *we*. Its mutuality opens up another field, more compelling if possible even than that of the persona, and moved by its own dynamic. In the *temenos* of the *we* there is no sense of needing to "fit in" and play an appropriate role, as in the persona field. Rather, we find ourselves already participating in a oneness that seems to belong to a deeper structure of the world than that of society's expectations. Social conventions seem inessential, arbitrary, and fleeting compared with this greater, more eternal reality of our erotic mutuality. We glimpse the unitary nature of the world and all the seemingly separate beings that comprise it. Our *we* is an instance of this supraordinate unity which I call the "self field."

The *self* of the "self field" derives from Jung's multivalent descriptions of "self" as the "center and circumference" of the whole personality, comprising the ego and its consciousness as well as the much greater reality of the unconscious. Jung's "self" is also "the eternal rhizome," the root structure out of which each individual personality springs as "the flower and fruit of a season." (Jung, 1912/ 52, pp. xxiv, f.)

"Self," is therefore the deepest, most complete, and central reality of each individual psyche as well as the transpersonal ground uniting every individual with every other. To speak of a "self field" is to name our experience in an erotic *temenos*, as participating in a *we* that undergirds the persisting reality of our separate *I* and *you*. It refers to our recognition that the *I* and the *you* find their fulfillment in and communicate through the *we*.

The term *field* evokes the image of a spatial locale subject to invisible forces like those of electro-magnetism. This suits very well the notion of a persona field in which our thoughts and expectations for ourselves fall into socially determined patterns like iron filings above a horseshoe magnet. The forces of the self field have a similar but deeper influence. They are the reason why a baby's cry can cause its mother's milk to flow, why lovers often seem able to read one another's minds, why disturbed patients may have such an uncanny ability to zero in on their therapists' secret weaknesses, and why individuals with a very amorphous sense of self may enjoy a euphoric feeling of wholeness in the presence of their therapists. The erotic *temenos* is therefore an interpersonal realm of great power in which the *we* exerts influences generally deemed unthinkable according to the Cartesian assumptions of our present-day persona field.

The realm of public discourse above all takes our separateness from one another as a fundamental given and holds up the ideal of personal independence as a central criterion of maturity. In doing so, our contemporary persona field down-plays the ineluctable fact that our lives as individuals are always interdependent with others.

We are social beings from birth to grave and discover our unique selves, indeed, only through interpersonal entanglements. Before birth we share the physiology and psychology of our mother. In our earliest years we are imbedded in a family reality which not only gives us our not-yet personal meaning as co-constituents of this small, all-important unit but actually defines and interprets the world for us. Our being-in-the-world is in the first instance a familial mode of existence. When we have achieved enough self-sufficiency to wander outside the home and play with other children, we bring our familial world along with us, for it defines the only *I* we have known.

As small children playing in the streets, playgrounds, or day-care centers of our neighborhoods, we find our being-in-the-family-world challenged by the lifeworlds of our playmates. We may fall into confusion about our identity or about the nature of the world, perplexed at the differences between the "family me" and the "playmate me." At each stage of our lives, we find ourselves imbedded in social worlds where our independent identity is more an abstract ideal than a self-evident reality. We discover our strengths, weaknesses, and possibilities in interchange with other people. Our very uniqueness is in large part a social achievement.

In all these situations that follow one another and overlap each other our whole life long, the sense of being a part of a *we* is a constant, foundational reality, even though it generally fades to the background of our attention. But when we find ourselves in an erotic *temenos*, *we-ness* jumps to the foreground as an issue of primary concern.

Insofar as this experience is a novelty for us, we may be struck first by all that is unknown in our entanglement with another. The *we* may fascinate us as portending a world of mystery, as the not-yet-lived and yearning-to-be-lived. But underlying this compelling opportunity for exploration is the inchoate awareness that something radically different has been revealed. We know we are approaching something as old as humanity and yet arcane, something that has not been discussed despite its lying open as the unacknowledged ground of all our prior taken-for-granted interactions.

We find ourselves confronted with the fact of our essential entangledness with one another and with the world at large. We have an almost "animistic" intimation of the unity of all beings. We understand for perhaps the first time why the mystics in all religious traditions reach for the language of Eros to describe their experience and why human lovers speak so mystically.

In the atmosphere of our presentday persona field, it is dangerous to speak of such things. It is a little as though we were standing on a street corner with a supply of LSD in our pocket, looking for buyers. To talk matter-of-factly of what it feels like to dwell in the fields of Venus is to seem to condone and even advocate "sexual acting out" between therapist and patient. That we leap so easily to such fearful conclusions is evidence of our "complex," our inability to avoid absolutism and fuzziness in our attitude toward "sexualizing" the therapeutic field.

Virtually every school of therapy since Freud agrees that stereotyped thinking about a subject betrays an "unresolved issue" and requires airing. Psychotherapists as a rule, however, have spoken of the erotic *temenos* only from the outside and primarily in the language of pathology: "fusion," "lack of boundaries," "psychotic countertransference," and "lack of self structure." While there is a great deal of truth in these metaphors and no doubt that Eros is a dangerous friend, this is no reason to close our eyes to the phenomenological facts about erotic relationships. It behooves us, therefore, to "bracket" the issue of sex a little while longer and consider what Eros itself has to offer when it enters the space between two people.

There is no set of commentators on the erotic field more painstaking in their descriptions than the religious mystics. They have embraced Eros unreservedly but with critical attention to every nuance of their experience. Their accounts have been written primarily for an audience already seriously concerned with matters erotic—as a kind of guide for finding one's way on the path to union in a *we* shared with God. In her *Interior Castle*,[5] Teresa of Avila articulates seven "mansions," or stations, along the way to divine union. John of the Cross, in *The Dark Night of the Soul*, speaks of three: early enthusiasm, the "Dark Night," and "infused contemplation."[6] Nelson Pike's phenomenological analysis of divine union distinguishes four typical stages in Christian mysticism: the "Prayer of Quiet," "Full Union," "Rapture," and "Union without Distinction." (Pike, 1992.)

Because these are carefully worded experiential accounts of what men and women have met in their progressively deepening encounters with the *we* they share with God, they are descriptions of *human* experience. They lay out for us, as no other literature does, the possibilities lurking in any numinous *we*. They describe in detail what we psychotherapists have been loath to approach, out of fear of falling afoul of the persona field. The mystics have been more courageous than we, daring to flirt with doctrinal heresy and excommunication in order to affirm the monumental facts of the erotic *temenos*.

Just as mysticism discovers the secret source and motivating truth of all religion, so the erotic field serves as the unacknowledged foundation of all therapeutic work. For this reason it is instructive to consider Pike's four stages in some detail and apply them to the *we* that may come to presence between a therapist and patient. Such an exercise goes a long way, I believe, toward demonstrating that "the

[5] I have applied these to human erotic relationships in *Divine Madness*, pp. 141-4.
[6] Cf. *Divine Madness*, pp. 35-7.

sexual" is not simply the literal meaning of "the erotic," as the persona field presses us to concede.

Stage One, the *Prayer of Quiet*, implies two prior degrees of religious consciousness which Pike does not discuss. The average believer, who perhaps prays for Aunt Alice to be cured of her cancer, "talks to God" even though *we-ness* has not emerged as an issue. Such an individual may worship regularly and observe all the doctrinal rules in total ignorance of anything like a divine Eros.

On the other hand, the earnest quester after mystical experience, perhaps through following a monastic life, must have had some personal intimation that a loving *we* can establish a mystical *temenos* and that the goal of living in that sacred space deserves priority over all the concerns of the public world. The renowned mystics have addressed their writings to this latter group, holding out the stages Pike has identified as landmarks along the path.

Applying these categories to psychological work, we have no trouble comparing the "average believer" to the psychotherapy client who perhaps wishes only to be relieved of a persistent anxiety which turns social encounters into ghastly trials. If such a patient feels comfortable enough to speak freely with the therapist, we know that a trusting *we* has been established even though *we-ness* itself has not stepped to the fore and may never be addressed. Erotic energy remains in the background, as the unacknowledged foundation of the work.

For the "earnest quester," however, the *we* has become an issue, as it has for the patient whose *we-ness* with a therapist can no longer be ignored. Whether such an individual takes delight in the therapist's presence or struggles with disturbances the therapeutic relationship brings about in a long-established self-image, the erotic nature of the *temenos* has emerged unmistakably. As the *we* assumes more and more importance, the relevance of the phenomenology of mysticism grows.

One of Pike's instances of the *Prayer of Quiet* is drawn from Teresa's "Fourth Mansion":

If this soul *burns with desire*, if she *prays without ceasing*, if her whole being goes out towards the Word, then suddenly it seems that she hears His voice *without seeing Him*; that is she savors *inwardly* the odor of His Divinity, which thing often comes to whose who are strong of faith. Suddenly the soul's *sense of smell* is filled with spiritual grace, and being aware of a sweet breath that tells her of the presence of Him whom she seeks, she says: Behold Him whom I *seek* and whom I *desire* (Pike, 1992, p. 50).

Here, the divine-human *we* has undeniably taken center stage; and the possibility of union in that *we* has shoved aside all other concerns. As close as the soul seems to be to God, however, it is still her *distance* from her Beloved that dominates her consciousness. Thus Teresa speaks of the soul's "distance senses," hearing and smell. She evokes the image of a lover exploring a large house in the dark, certain her beloved is somewhere close, perhaps in the next room; for she can hear his voice and smell his after-shave.

Union is tantalizingly near but hardly an accomplished fact. Above all, sight is lacking—the most dependable of the five senses. Yet, though her soul is "still in the dark," the nearness of what she hears and smells provides no little satisfaction. Prior to the Prayer of Quiet, uncertainties and distractions from the *we* were regular occurrences. Now, however, nothing can undermine the soul's confidence.

When this confidence is reached in psychotherapy, it is no longer adequate to say that clinician and patient take delight in their work and enjoy one another's presence. The *we* has assumed a much greater importance as the place of imminent union in which my *I* and your *you* can find both dissolution and fulfillment. We are no longer merely collaborating in a work to resolve the neurotic "hang-ups" from which one of us suffers. The *we* has brought our relationship itself into focus as our central occupation.

If formerly we faded in and out concern for our *we-ness*, we can no longer tolerate such waffling; for our confidence is unshakable that an enlarging, transformative union is at hand. Perhaps the patient

hopes to gain confidence and stability from the therapist's more secure and coherent sense of self. Perhaps the therapist expects an
increase in openness and flexibility from the patient's more boundless and protean self. But such hopes remain secondary to their concern
with the *we* which defines and dominates their mutual self field.

Pike illustrates the stage of *Full Union* with the following passage
from the *Revelations* of Angela of Foligno:

> And beyond this the soul receives the gift of seeing God. God says to
> her "Behold Me!" and the soul sees Him dwelling within her. She sees
> Him more clearly than one man sees another. For *the eyes of the soul
> behold a plentitude of which I cannot speak: a plentitude which is not bodily
> but spiritual, of which I can say nothing.* And the soul rejoices in that
> sight with an ineffable joy; and this is the manifest and certain sign
> that God dwells in her (Pike, 1992, p. 56).

I have chosen to cite this account, out of the several Pike presents,
because I find it to be the shortest and clearest. Nevertheless it is
unique in singling out the sense of "spiritual sight." The others emphasize taste and touch. They all agree, however, that God dwells
within the soul and describe this with sensory metaphors that insist a
former distance has been overcome. Whether I contemplate God inside me with the "eyes of the soul," savor God with my "soul's tongue,"
or feel God pressing against me with my "soul's skin," there is no
space between us. We are together in the *we*. The "nearness senses" of
taste, touch, and sight are meant to convince us that union is an
accomplished fact, even though greater union is still possible.

The soul has moved from the certainty that union is attainable and
imminent to the enjoyment of oneness in the *we*. The mystics emphasize the ineffability of this experience: *the eyes of the soul behold . . . a
plentitude which is not bodily but spiritual.* Angela means that though she
has no words but those devised publicly and used in everyday discourse,
she wishes to point to an experience wholly foreign to the assumptions
of the persona field. The "eyes of the soul" gaze upon "non-ordinary"
realities, those that come to presence only in the erotic *temenos*.

For therapist and patient to move from the certain imminence of invisible union to its "taste" and "sight," means they have found the *we* not only as an opportunity to approach but as a reality already working its effects upon them. They have advanced from the stage of separate beings who find one another interesting (emergence of the *we*) through the stage of circumambulating the *we* (Prayer of Quiet) to the stage of cohabiting the *we*. While retaining their distinct identities, they influence one another at the level of "soul," or self.

One feels the other's fragmentation and incoherence, perhaps, as a gentle, loosening pressure, an opening, that is clearly *yours* but nevertheless a possibility for *me*. If so, the second (the patient) responds in a reciprocal manner, finding the solidity and security of the therapist not just as an insight but as a reality seen with unaccustomed eyes. The patient "feels" and "tastes" the therapist's self, savoring it as belonging to the uniqueness of the *you* and sensing its soulful sway as a gentle inducement toward finding a centeredness that is distinctively *mine*. Very likely they have no words for this experience. They only know that the *temenos* of the self field generates events for which the familiarities of the persona world have left them entirely unprepared.

To illustrate the stage of *Rapture*, Pike cites a passage from Angela of Foligno's *Visions and Instructions*:

> On one occasion, however, my soul was lifted up . . . when it was in that darkness, wished to return to itself, and could not, wished to proceed and could not. Then suddenly it was lifted higher and enlightened, and it saw the unutterable *Power* of God, and it saw the *Will* of God and His *Justice* and *Goodness*, in which I most fully understood all the things about which I had asked [concerning the Fall of man and his Redemption]. . . . And I was so full of charity [*claritas*] and with such joy did I have understanding of the power and will and justice of God, and not only did I have knowledge of those things about which I had enquired, but I was also satisfied with regard to all things. But this I cannot make known in any words whatsoever, for it is wholly above nature (Pike, 192, p. 57).

If there is a "reality shift" as we move from the persona field to the erotic *temenos*, there is another equally jarring transition as one moves from Full Union to Rapture. Angela describes being transported, taken out of herself in an ecstasy, where she experiences a kind of catalepsy of the soul: *wished to return to itself, and could not, wished to proceed and could not.* Her soul has fallen into a sublime trance in which she is done to and no longer doing. Here marvelous things are revealed to her. She comes to know God not just as the Other who cohabits the divine-human *we* with her, but the very facets of God's godhood (power, will, justice, goodness).

In a later passage she speaks of coming to see the Holy Trinity: *yet at such a time I see all things, and see nothing* (p. 58). This is a very unusual kind of "seeing," not like anything encountered heretofore in the light of Eros. But just as the notion of *seeing* must be extended almost to non-sense to account for her immediate and certain kind of knowing, so also what is seen is both distinct and indistinct.

It is distinct in that she sees "all things" and indistinct in that she sees "nothing." I take this to mean that she has seen the unity of all things, whereby she sees everything in a single glance. In seeing everything, she sees no single thing in its distinctness as separate from everything else. Yet by seeing the particulars in their unity, she sees more essentially and appreciates more deeply.

Rapture in psychotherapy is very similar to what the mystic of Foligno has described. One finds oneself taken over and shifted into a new way of seeing in which the *we* retains its centrality but one is impressed above all by the unitary nature of reality. As in all erotic ways of seeing, we have no conscious means to induce rapturous experience. It comes upon us unbidden.

If the previous states seem gradual so that the demarcations between them are hard to draw, rapture brings with it the sense of a sudden rupture of plane. One moment we are in the *we*, savoring the flavors and feeling the pressures of Full Union; in the next we are transported, almost levitated as in a glowing ball of light, where everything becomes clearer and yet more fuzzy.

The ball seems to be the *we* itself, in which *I* and *you* remain distinct while jointly constituting a unity that is as equally valid and real as our separate selves. In this state we contemplate simultaneously—without (as it were) turning our heads—the *you-ness* of you, the *I-ness* of me, and the unitary nature of the world.

I have had an experience like this on several occasions, and can report that Angela of Foligno's claim to have come to know the facets of God's godhead (power, justice, goodness, etc.) corresponds very well with what I have learned about my partner in the *temenos* of the self field. I enjoy a certainty that I am perceiving my partner's selfhood in its many faceted unity—as though I know the facets intimately, but only as participating in their unity.

Everything and nothing is seen. We come back with little to say, but changed in our relationship to one another. We are sure we know this *you* deeply and in detail, but we do not know how to begin to put words to it. To doubt what we have learned is impossible, and subsequent experience in ordinary space and time only confirms the accuracy of what we have gained. New events may surprise us in their particulars, but the essential truth we have seen in our self-field rapture is not controverted but enriched.

Pike's highest stage, *Union without Distinction*, may be illustrated with a passage from Jan van Ruysbroeck's *The Sparkling Stone*:

> The union with God which a spiritual man feels, when the union is revealed to the spirit as being abysmal, [is one in which the spirit] feels itself to be wandering in the breadth, and to dwell in a knowledge which is ignorance. And through this intimate feeling of union, it feels itself to be melting into the Unity; and, through dying to all things, into the life of God. And there it feels itself to be one life with God. . . . In the transformation within the Unity, all spirits fail in their own activity, and feel nothing else but a burning up of themselves in the simple Unity of God. . . . In this transcendent state the spirit feels in itself the eternal fire of love. . . . The spirit forever continues to burn in itself, for its love is eternal; and it feels itself ever

more and more to be burnt up in love, for it is drawn and transported into the Unity of God, where the spirit burns in love. If it observes itself, it finds a distinction and an otherness between itself and God; but where it is burnt up it is undifferentiated and without distinction, and therefore it feels nothing but unity; for the flame of the Love of God consumes and devours all that it can enfold in its Self (Pike, 1992, pp. 154f).

Van Ruysbroeck begins with what we already know about the stage of Rapture, thereby implying that Union without Distinction occurs as an extension of the earlier state. What develops is precisely what we imagined as the goal of erotic union back when the *we* first emerged, that we were being "called" to dissolve or "melt" into one another, to become *one* without distinction.

Pike struggles a great deal to imagine how this can be, that there is an undifferentiated *one* and yet still enough of a *me* that I can contemplate it. He comes up with an analogy involving two stories. In the first, I am hit in the head with a baseball while sitting on a park bench reading a newspaper and immediately pass out. Because I had not seen what hit me, I have nothing to report upon regaining consciousness but, "Stun-stars and fading consciousness." This is how it would be if I were to dissolve in God without appreciating the events leading up to it.

But if I have set aside the newspaper and seen the baseball arcing toward my forehead, I will have a different report when I regain consciousness: "I was hit with a baseball." The mystics know they were hit with the "baseball" of divine union because they have been standing in the field with their gloves on, playing the mystical game. They know what preceded their dissolution, so they experience their burning up in God as the end result of a process. It is not just going unconscious, it is reaching the goal of the abyss (*union . . . as being abysmal*).

We can only conclude that the abyss of ego-dissolution which *is* Union without Distinction, is also marked by a blissfulness that sets it apart from "stun-stars and fading consciousness."

If I have had any experience of Union without Distinction in the context of psychotherapy it was extremely impoverished in comparison with van Ruysbroeck's. There was one occasion in which I experienced my body becoming entirely comprised of flame. I was not burning, not in pain (which John of the Cross insists upon), perceived no heat; and I did not feel I was melting into my analysand. She was too frightened of union for me to have asked her for a report on her sensations.

What was prominent, however, was that we were both coming up with the same images and the same ideas at the same time. Perhaps there was some kind of mental "non-distinction." But, ever the analyst, I could not resist putting interpretive twists on my presentation of some of the images, little baseball-glove hints at where we had gotten to and where we had been. Perhaps these deliberate ego-guided moves brought a premature end to the union. In any event, I could not determine it had any noticeable effects upon the course of our work—although it changed *me*. I became more deeply convinced of the homology between human erotic experience and the reports of the mystics.

Jung speaks of something like this in *The Psychology of the Transference* (Jung, 1946), although the writing is quite opaque, being a commentary on a series of woodcuts from an alchemical text of the sixteenth century. "The Conjunction," which pictures a winged couple in sexual embrace, is the central image in a process where, "Doctor and patient find themselves in a relationship founded on mutual unconsciousness" (par. 364). Jung cautions that the picture must not be seen as pornography but symbolism: "Union on the biological level is a symbol of the *unio oppositorum* at its highest level" (par. 460).

Still, "The reader should not imagine the psychologist is in any position to explain what `higher copulation' is" (par. 465). He is dubious about the possibility of "resolving the transference"—by which he apparently means diminishing the erotic pull, placing limits on the unitive moment in Eros. Because "the unconscious insists upon it" and "things cannot be forced" (par. 463), we have no choice but to follow the call of the *we*, while keeping our eyes and ears open for the dangers that will certainly abound.

It would be unreasonable to think that Jung, in his extremely guarded circumspection, is not referring to his own experience; for we know that he became sexually involved with at least two of his patients (Sabina Spielrein and Toni Wolff) and that those relationships became definitive for his conception of analysis.

Given Jung's refusal to speak openly, we have no recourse but to observe the place "Conjunction" occupies in the context of the whole work. It is the fifth stage in a ten-part process, implying that the work is only half done when therapist and patient find themselves in a Union without Distinction. In the remaining woodcuts, there are no longer two figures but one, half male and half female. Thus the union, so far from being a passing incident, continues as a constant to the end of the work. In woodcuts six through nine, the hermaphrodite that symbolizes the union of therapist and patient, lies dead in its coffin, an image of extreme unconsciousness, even depression. After the transporting bliss of union, everything falls dead; and the efforts of analysis involve preparing the body for the return of the soul and the rebirth of the "new being," also an hermaphrodite.

All of this suggests that we cannot take Union without Distinction as the goal of erotic work. It is but the high point in a process that must continue. There is, however, one more ideal we can accept from the mystics. We know that Union without Distinction did not last forever. They had to get on with their daily lives, had to eat and sleep, had to administer their monasteries, and in many cases had to argue theology with the religious authorities of their day—mystical writings always being a dangerous undertaking that arouses suspicions of heresy and subversion.

Ignatius of Loyola, who experienced all the stages of mystical union and found they tended to interfere with his practical activities, made it a maxim for his Jesuit Order that every member should be a "contemplative in action." Formal time set aside for contemplation, when one might occasionally enjoy one of the advanced states of Union, are to be limited to an hour or two per day. While opportunities for extraordinary experiences of the divine Eros are limited, the individual Jesuit is urged to take with him into his daily concerns a lively awareness of God's presence.

What is imagined, here, is a life conducted as an erotic partnership with God. Unlike couples in the first blush of their enthusiasm, these divine lovers leave the connubial bed of their oratory to labor in the world. And unlike bored spouses, they retain their transformative *we-ness* throughout the day until they can deepen it with undivided attention when they return at night.

In similar fashion, therapist and patient may carry into the every-day work of analysis an awareness of union: a union revealed in its profundity through its peak moments, but potentially effective dur-ing sessions in which lethargy, deadness, depression, and misunderstandings dominate our mutual consciousness.

Now that we have considered the erotic field in its many forms, from the most common and rudimentary to the loftiest and most rar-efied, we can remove the "brackets" from sexuality to see what it brings to an interpersonal *temenos* characterized by a numinous *we*.

At the outset we have to admit the inaccuracy of our naive desire to distinguish "the erotic" from "the sexual"—as though the *we* could ever be unbodied. Even the mystics, whom we can hardly suspect of "sexualizing" religion, speak of bodily sensations and describe "the soul" in bodily language. They commonly use frankly sexual terms for divine union. It is hardly unthinkable that they may sometimes have displayed physiological signs of sexual arousal during their encoun-ters with God. Certainly erectile and mucosal changes would not be rare between a therapist and patient experiencing powerful erotic forces during their sessions. Very likely hormones are released during even the milder kinds of erotic encounter.

Beyond this, we must consider imaginal sensations of the body. We say our "heart opens," and we mean it metaphorically, but we actually seem to feel our chest opening sometimes in a powerful erotic *temenos*; or it may be our belly or our whole trunk from pubis to throat. Eastern mystics speak of openings in the throat, forehead, and crown; and we can hardly imagine they mean these sensations in a different way than we do.

We say we are "filled with energy" when we feel a boundless enthusiasm; but we may be referring to an actual bodily sensation, that we feel like a vessel bursting with the pressure of an overabundance of energy. Perhaps we feel we are vibrating with an energy that does not know where to go. We may also feel it flowing, up from our feet and out through the "opening" in our chest or at the top of our head. Sometimes we are sure that it is flowing between us: in one direction, from one partner to the other; or cycling through us both.

There may well be a sexual flavor to any of these sensations. But *insofar as they come unbidden and are observed and tolerated without our fastening on them, emphasizing them, or "acting them out,"* we may locate them in the realm of "the erotic" rather than in that of "the sexual." We want to keep a substantial distinction between these two terms, *erotic* and *sexual*; for the one is essential to our work while the other is highly questionable. Fuzzy areas abound and would suck us into absolutism, into throwing out "the erotic" with "the sexual" (as the persona field presses us to do). As though *we-ness*, in one form or another, were not the very ground of therapy.

Because "the erotic" is so dangerously close to "the sexual" and often enough involves sexual feelings and sensations as part of its own proper dynamic, it seems reasonable to locate what we call "the sexual" in *our attitude toward those feelings and sensations*. Sexual feelings may arise at any time in an erotic *temenos*. When we can observe them as natural elements of the interpersonal field in the same way we identify child-parent feelings, novice-mentor feelings, and the like, they become evidence of a specific quality in our psychic interactions and call for interpretation.

They are dangerous only to the extent that they throw us off course, make us lose our therapeutic stance, and preoccupy us unduly. This is generally what we mean when we speak of "the sexual" in the context of psychotherapy: a disruptive, riveting, fascination that would induce us to engage in lovemaking of various kinds: titillating conversation, caresses, genital intercourse.

Outside the purely soul-oriented erotic realm of the mystics, sexual expression seems to be the natural form for erotic feelings. It promises a bodily union that would actualize in a concrete manner the "call" of the *we*. So obviously does sex seem to follow this "call," that few of our contemporaries can imagine any other way of responding. This is, in fact, the reason "the erotic" has been collapsed into "the sexual" in public discourse. For when we have not yet discerned the *we* and the self field it opens, we have no other category by which to grasp this feeling of being drawn toward dissolution with another.

After having surveyed the topography of the erotic field, we can appreciate the fact that sexuality might have as many meanings as there are stations along the path to union. Furthermore, it seems obvious that "sexualizing" an encounter might take it in either of two ways. Sexual enactment might *halt* the erotic process, if it directs our attention away from the *we* to our bodily sensations and social conquests. Or it might *intensify* the process and enable us to appreciate our *we-ness* in greater depth and finer detail.

Let us "bracket" the issue of psychotherapy for a time and consider the relationship between "the sexual" and "the erotic" a little further—as purely *human* possibilities. Later we can apply our observations to the therapeutic field.

We have already concluded that the man who responds to the ad for telephone sex described in the introduction to this chapter has no interest at all in a *we*. He hopes only that the woman behind the ad will play an exciting role and assist his achieving orgasm. It would not be sufficient, however, to imagine that he craves only "his own pleasure," as though the physiological accompaniments of ejaculation were all that interest him.

In choosing a "sex-starved nympho," he may be seeking someone as insatiable as he feels himself to be, someone who will respect his own starvation. Or possibly he fears that only a woman whose appetite for sex is uncontrollable would accept an approach from someone like himself. We also note that he wants "raw, nasty sex." It would be reasonable to guess that he experiences sex as an anti-social activity, something dirty and belonging to barnyards and back alleys.

If this is true, he may believe himself unfit for everyday human society unless he can keep his shameful impulses under tight control. Dialing the number in the ad may be his way of throwing off the strictures of a narrow and overly compulsive life. Or it may itself the the compulsion he longs to be rid of. Surely every man who calls that number has psychological reasons for doing so, as well as physiological.

When the *we* comes to presence between two people, more may be expected of sex. We do not overlook the fact that physical pleasure and ego-centered psychological concerns can reassert themselves at the first frankly sexual gesture, distracting us from the *we* and turning the *you* into a commodity for *me*. It is public knowledge that the physical dimensions of sex can be so overwhelming, that our level of consciousness may be drastically lowered and our attention held captive to instinctuality.

But the energies of bodily sexuality can also be directed *in service* of the *we*. Eros can be intensified, as the *we* calls more urgently and hidden dimensions of the *you* are unveiled. Sexuality might sometimes be an engine that moves us from one station to the next on the track of erotic union.

When *we-ness* lurks in the background of our meetings, inspiring interest in one another and generating joy in our mutual presence, sexuality may stir. Our familiarity and comfort with one another may suggest the possibility of enhancing our companionship by enacting it in a physical manner. In order not to lose sight of the unique *you* before us, a sexual approach will surely bring the *we* into the foreground of our attention.

For whenever sex is a giving of myself to you in which both the *I* and the *you* are maintained and affirmed, the *we* is inevitably brought to the fore as the location and possibility of our meeting. In similar manner sexual involvement may move us from the merely fascinating *we* of lower-level erotic fields to the unshakable certainty of the Prayer of Quiet's "distance senses," thence to "tasting" and "feeling" the *you* in the *we* of Full Union and on to the unitary detail of "ignorant" knowing in Rapture before experiencing the "melting" of Union without Distinction.

If we now remove the "brackets" from the issue of psychotherapy, we find ourselves faced with two likely conclusions: one safe and com-

forting, the other dangerous and alarming. First the comforting conclusion: Eros, which we have described as "the ground and life of
therapy," may be truncated, brought to a halt, and diverted from its
course by the introduction of "the sexual." In this regard we have no
trouble rejecting sexuality from the therapeutic *temenos*; and we
breathe a sigh of relief, knowing we thereby place ourselves solidly in
harmony with the ethics of the persona field.

But this is only one class of sexual experience. Although it may be
the most common form, its definition ("sexuality as a distraction from
our *we-ness*") leaves open the opposite possibility. This is our alarming conclusion: "the sexual" may sometimes enhance "the erotic" by
contributing to the "call" and guidance of the *we*.

If we accept the phenomenon of sexual enhancement in an erotic
field, and insist that Eros belongs to therapy as its "ground and life,"
we seem to have painted ourselves into a dangerous and untenable
corner *vis-a-vis* the passionately held morality of the public world. For
if we leave the door ajar to sexual expression in the context of psychotherapy, we seem to countenance the very abuses we hear decried
and condemned from all sides.

Surely there is a very real possibility that the self-deluded as well as
out-and-out opportunists may seize upon our argument to justify
"sexual acting out" in its most destructive forms. This is in fact what
motivates public discourse to take such an absolute and unyielding
position: *any aspect of sex in the context of therapy is always wrong.*

Although it is unnerving to find ourselves on the "wrong side" of
such an inflammatory issue, we might well decide to "tough it out" if
we have none but the self-deluded and opportunistic to worry about.
For these individuals do not need a closely observant analysis of the
erotic field to justify going their own way.

Our dilemma is more difficult than that. We are concerned about
the sincere and self-critical few who are cautiously following the guidance of the *we*. Do we wish to encourage them to employ sexual
methods to enhance the erotic process in certain kinds of therapeutic
field? Have we not argued—at least outside the context of therapy—
that sex may be a dangerous but perhaps useful tool? If so, what is to

exclude it from the therapeutic *temenos*? We have advanced no argument to do so.

At the same time, however, we have made no argument in *favor* of employing "the sexual" as an enhancement of *therapeutic* Eros. We have arrived only at two conclusions and not yet questioned the relationship they may have with one another. The first is that sexuality may sometimes assist the *generally human* course of erotic union—for instance in the forum of marriage.

Regarding therapy, we have only said that Eros is its "ground and life." We have not identified Eros as the *goal* of therapy. Indeed, in considering the role of the "Conjunction" in Jung's *Psychology of the Transference*, we have found that Union without Distinction may very well be merely the mid-point of the therapeutic process. We have made no inquiry into what therapeutic stages might follow such a union. Above all, we have said nothing about the "goal" of therapy. It would surely be unwarranted to assume therapy has the same goal as marriage.

Before we can draw any conclusions about the appropriateness of Eros-enhancing sex for the psychotherapeutic endeavor, we require an investigation into the aims of therapy. This will be the topic of the next two chapters. This will give us a temporary reprieve from contemplating the dangerous conclusion we seem to have come so close to making.

Four

The Love Cure Part I:

*The Love They Had
Longed for as Children*

Love has been both the transformative secret and the Achilles heel of psychoanalysis from its very earliest days, for erotic rapport lies at the heart of the work. On December 6, 1906, Freud wrote to Jung of the essential doctrine:

> Transference provides the impulse necessary for understanding and translating the language of the ucs [unconscious]; where it is lacking, the patient does not make the effort or does not listen when we submit our translation to him. Essentially, one might say, the cure is effected by love. And actually transference provides the most cogent, indeed, the only unassailable proof that neuroses are determined by the individual's love life (McGuire, 1974, pp. 12f).

In this passage the love that effects the cure is the *patient's*. In the erotic *temenos* of the therapeutic field, the patient is "taken with" the analyst—as with a parent or lover—leading to the benefits of effort and docility.

Although similar observations had already been made by Charcot and Janet a decade and more earlier, neither they nor Freud spoke of their own response to the patient. Can we believe it had not yet occurred to them? It surely *had* occurred to Breuer, who fled to the mountains to escape his infatuation with Anna O. At the time of Freud's "love cure" letter, Jung was already preoccupied with a twenty-year-old Russian Jewish student suffering from "psychotic hysteria," named Sabina Spielrein. According to her diary he had drafted an account of his problematic work with her in an unposted letter to his future mentor some nine months before the Freud/Jung correspondence began. (Carotenuto, 1982, p. 101). Furthermore,

> Jung was scarcely the only person to become involved with a patient. Gross' exploits were legendary, Stekel had long enjoyed a reputation as a "seducer," Jones was paying blackmail money to a former patient, and even the good Pastor Pfister was lately entranced by one of his charges. Indeed, the most extraordinary entanglement was Ferenczi's, the amiable Hungarian having taken into analysis the daughter of the woman he was having an affair with and then fallen in love with the girl. Freud in fact was [in fall, 1910] seeing the younger woman at Ferenczi's request in an attempt to rescue the situation (Kerr, 1992, p. 379).

Love was so much the concern of psychoanalysis that Freud repudiated Adler, saying: "He has created for himself a world system without love, and I am in the process of carrying out on him the revenge of the offended goddess Libido" (Roazen, 1976, p. 186). Freud and Jung themselves had powerfully erotic relationships with their closest associates, many of whom had been in analysis with them. Jung's were mostly of the opposite sex, and his wife complained to Freud, "Naturally the women are all in love with him" (McGuire, 1974, p. 467). Freud, on the other hand, tended to form intense friendships with men that ended in acrimony resembling the enmity of separated lovers (Fliess, Breuer, Jung, Tausk, etc.). Jung wrote frankly of Freud's erotic effects upon himself shortly after their first meeting:

> I have got the feeling of having made considerable inner progress since I got to know you personally; it seems to me that one can never understand your science unless one knows you in the flesh. Where so

much still remains dark to us outsiders only faith can help; but the best and most effective faith is knowledge of your personality. Hence my visit to Vienna was a genuine confirmation (McGuire, p. 30).

That Freud's friendship with Ferenczi did not end in a lovers' tiff probably speaks to the latter's amiable submission. Setting aside Otto Gross on the basis of his instability (he had recommended his own practice of overcoming sexual repression through free love), Ferenczi was the most outspoken of the earliest analysts on the encouragement of Eros in the transference field. He argued for "changes in the direction of 'elasticity' and 'relaxation'" and the "ability to meet a patient at least half way, to make of the therapeutic relationship a genuine interpersonal encounter" (Roazen, 1976, p. 363).

Freud agreed that, "One could effect far more with one's patients if one gave them enough of the love which they had longed for as children" (Roazen, 1976, p. 363f). Yet he was worried about Ferenczi's practice of kissing his patients and allowing them to kiss him, fearing it would lead to sexual involvement (Roazen, 1976, p. 367).

To stop at the fact that our present-day preoccupation with the issue of sex in psychotherapy has long ignoble past, would be to see only the superficial aspect of the issue. It deserves more serious consideration. We need to grasp how it is that therapists from Freud onward have been fascinated with the idea that *the cure is effected by love.* Freud provides two important rationales. He gives the first in his 1906 letter to Jung: *where it is lacking, the patient does not make the effort or does not listen when we submit our translation to him.*

Pierre Janet (1889) had already remarked upon this phenomenon, calling it, somewhat less dramatically, the patient's "need to be directed" (*besoin de direction*). For Janet this is the defining characteristic of all neurosis as well as the handle by which the therapist grabs hold of the patient to effect change and lead him to psychic health. Furthermore, the disappearance of the *besoin de direction*, provides undeniable evidence that the cure has been effective and insures the patient will not cling to the therapist any longer than necessary.[1]

---

[1] For a discussion of Janet's theory of transference, cf. Haule, 1986.

More recently Harold Searles (1959) has made a similar observation: "Time after time [in] . . . a thorough-going analytic cure, I have experienced romantic and erotic desires to marry, and fantasies of being married to the patient." He goes on to say that it is often important to allow the patient to see how deeply affected the analyst has become; and the success of the cure is demonstrated by therapist and patient "working through" their mutual fantasy of marriage before termination.

Although Searles adds subjective testimony about his own feelings that Freud and Janet ignored or concealed, he is in essential agreement with them in treating "transference love" as providing the atmosphere in which, alone, therapy can be successful. Love binds us together in a common work that feels vitally significant. Our very lives are entwined, as in marriage. Therapy is an erotic enterprise demanding a kind of union in which both parties undergo a partial dissolution and interpenetration, much as we experience in romantic love. The work itself is not love but takes place within an interpersonal field created and nourished by love. Eros is the ground and life of the work.

Freud says something rather different, however, in his support of Ferenczi: *One could effect far more with one's patients if one gave them enough of the love which they had longed for as children.* Here, love is more than a condition of effective therapy; it is the essential factor in psychological health. The patient has fallen ill because a natural childhood need for love has gone unfulfilled, resulting in an unrequited longing that lies behind all neurotic dissatisfactions. Such an individual may well be predisposed to love the therapist, inspired by a "need for direction." But more than this, her therapist will accomplish "far more" by "giving her enough of the love" for which she has been "longing."

The love they had longed for as children is surely not kindness and good intentions, nor is it demonstrated by gushing speeches about how beautiful, intelligent, charming, and lovable they may be. They do not want play-acting, they want *love*. They have had enough of "good intentions" and pats on the cheek. They want to be taken seriously.

They can no longer be bought with consolations and substitutions and are cynical about promises. They want the real thing, and will sniff suspiciously around it a good long time before they are satisfied they are not being duped again.

Their parents have treated them like objects, annoyances, animated toys to be put on display, treasures to be cooed over like dolls. Human beings need to be taken as persons. We want to be someone's *you*, to be valued for being the unique individuals we are. We want someone to know how we feel and to care about it. We want someone who will pay attention when we try to tell her who we think we are. We want her to tell us how we seem to her and to appreciate why we do what we do.

If she is willing and able to take us this seriously, we will be more than grateful. We will want to know who *she* is. We have never encountered anyone like this, and may well be suspicious that there is something "wrong" with her to find us interesting and valuable when the world has been telling us all our lives that we are not worthy of attention. But as soon as the worst of our doubts are allayed, a lively sense of *we-ness* emerges into the foreground of our attention. We find ourselves in an erotic *temenos*.

The cure is not effected by love because Freud, Ferenczi, and other early psychoanalysts declared it to be so and built a method around it, nor because they have had undue influence upon their followers. Love alone effects the cure because love is the only way we humans have for taking one another seriously. It gives us an interest sufficient to penetrate beneath the surface. Only when we value what we find in our patient do we wish to go on and on, traversing the byways and back alleys, exploring the chasms and climbing the peaks of his soul. No one has done this with him before, no one has found his inestimable *you-ness*. He has doubted its existence himself, despaired of finding it. Our *I* and his *you* emerge only out of the *we* that Eros brings to presence between us.

We do not have to have read Freud or to have idealized Jung's forty-year-long relationship with his former patient, Toni Wolff, to come to the conclusion that *the cure is effected by love*. This truth lurks within every therapeutic relationship that works. Even if we fail to bring it thematically to consciousness, we use it every day in our practice. Eros is the power source that sparks our meetings and gives them the juice we need. We root in vain through our tool kit of techniques when a lively sense of *we-ness* does not at least occupy the background of our therapeutic field. True enough, it may remain unacknowledged as the taken-for-granted foundation of our work, inspiring interest and urgency, but not stepping to the fore as our primary concern.

We are eager to agree with Jung in his *Psychology of the Transference* (1946, par. 359): "I am personally always glad when there is only a mild transference or when it is practically unnoticeable. Far less claim is then made upon one as a person, and one can be satisfied with other therapeutically effective factors."

For when *we-ness* obtrudes to the center of our mutual consciousness, we are entangled too deeply and fear the patient means too much to us. Our stability is called in question, and the need for transformation becomes as much an issue for us as for our patient. We find ourselves on shaky ground *vis-à-vis* the public world with its anxiety in the face of "the erotic" and "the sexual." We find it much more comfortable when Eros obligingly patrols the periphery of the therapeutic field. But we cannot get on without him.

Freud's observation about *the love they had longed for as children* refers to a primal experience, the unquestioned acceptance and security with which an adequate parent loves an infant dependent upon her in every way. If as adults they are still longing for this love, they evidently missed something very important, indeed. For if their parents have not loved them adequately, very likely no one has, and their personhood remains undiscovered. Never having been able to find security, they have never experienced the world as a safe place to be. They must be wholly afloat, at loose ends in a life that is chaotic both internally and externally. The center, that is to say the *self*, does not hold. They dream, perhaps, of riding in a bus without sides that spills its human cargo as it careens around corners. Chaotic emotions overwhelm, intimidate, and shatter them into fragments striving in contradictory directions. They have no peace and search for solace in the most self-destructive forms.

Above all, their relationships are in turmoil. Although unable to identify the central problem, they are obsessed with the love they have missed. Either they are so disillusioned about finding it that they wall themselves off from other people behind anger, cynicism, shyness, and self-defeat; or they throw themselves disastrously into one dependent relationship after another, finding unreliable mother- and father-figures everywhere who repeat the disappointments of their childhood. Possibly they "sexualize" their relationships potently in order to cement in physical union the bond they are looking for. Partner after partner finds them irresistible and then is driven away by an emotional tumult of resentment, fear, and possessiveness.

When we find ourselves enmeshed with a patient like this, feelings of responsibility and protectiveness overwhelm us; for our patient lives on the brink of annihilation or overwhelming existential anxiety and carries her fragmentary ego-hood as a burden that is slipping out of her grasp. Isolation, abandonment, and dissolution threaten constantly, and we both feel it. There may be moments when we feel superhumanly powerful and capable; and then, abruptly, we lose all sense of coherence, as our patient's insecurity infects us. In our weakness and confusion, we may feel that she has suddenly become our superior, dazzling in her wisdom, self-righteous in her rage. We are inadequate and foolish and wonder how we dare pose as a therapist.

Again, with dizzying speed, our roles reverse and we are the only one in her life solid enough and suitably gifted to contain the chaos that fills the interpersonal field between us. Because our patient's sense of being an *I* is rudimentary at best, no distinct experience of a *we* is possible; and our own strangely unreliable coherence has to do double duty, making *us* a person and providing *her* with a borrowed sense of stable personhood.

If we see such an individual accurately as the not-yet-person she is, we know precisely how and why she needs the love she had longed for as a child. She wants the security-giving affection that will enable her to discover her "self." She looks for it from us. But particularly when the atmosphere of the therapeutic field is "sexualized" by her needs and ours, we doubt the ethical propriety of giving it to her. We may even doubt our capacity to supply it. But if *we* do not provide her the love she longs for, who will? Do we have to reject her as unsuitable for therapy, thereby confirming in a perhaps final manner her greatest fear, that she is incapable and unworthy of joining the human community? We need some guidelines about how to provide that love in a way that has some hope of helping her to find the secure and coherent center she so badly needs, and without straying from the field of therapy into a deeper and more unconscious enmeshment.

In my view, Heinz Kohut's "self psychology" articulates those guidelines. Essentially he provides three principles. (a) The precondition for the work is an intense, lop-sided rapport between the nascent self of the patient and the coherent self of the therapist, in which the latter is accepted is a kind of substitute self or "self-object" that provides vicarious stability to the patient. (b) The work itself begins by gratifying the patient's need to be taken seriously through clear-sighted "empathy" that discerns and articulates ("mirrors") the emerging self of the patient as well as the emotional chaos that surrounds, confuses, and fragments him. (c) Most effective, however, are the necessary "frustrations" the therapist must give to the patient's inevitable demands for "inappropriate gratifications"—but "empathically," sorrowfully and with full emotional awareness of the desolation being caused ("optimal frustration").

Kohut has, in effect, described the nature of parental love in nuanced detail. What they longed for as children was to be seen for who they are, seen with the heart as well as the mind, valued, and enjoyed. But they also wanted to be corrected and shown their limits, with a compassion that is willing to share the pain as well as the joy of their inchoate struggling personhood. Parents express these things as they feed, bathe, and cuddle their infant, while a therapist is limited to seeing, feeling, and talking.

What adequate parents do spontaneously—for it is simply the way one loves an infant—the therapist needs a theory to justify. She has to be more conscious than the parent of her own feelings and those of the patient; and she has to be able to find the words, gestures, and tone of voice to convey what is going on "inside" the patient and within the therapeutic *temenos*. Therapeutic love for a self-in-becoming amounts to parental love that has been "thematized" (consciously understood in detail and as a whole).

In Kohut's view, *the self is effected by love*; and he calls this love "empathy." He refers to Freud's *cure through love* statement in a long footnote, where he applies it disapprovingly to "Jung's commanding personality which undoubtedly exerted a deep influence on his co-workers and thus, indirectly, on the severely disturbed patients in his therapeutic community." He calls it "a cure through . . . narcissistic love!" (1971, p. 223). He believes the missing element in Jung's work is precisely the thematizing that self psychology provides.

It is not hard to find both prongs of Freud's advocacy of "transference love" in Kohut's practice of therapy. The notion of self-object rapport is a more refined variation of *getting them to make the effort and to listen*; and empathy is a highly nuanced form of *giving the love they had longed for as children*.

Because there is no ground or substance to the "narcissistic" proto-ego, it immerses itself in the self-object sufficiency of the therapist—very much as a child who would be contained again within the womb, where its own physiology and psychology are indistinguishable from mother's. In a primitive manner, this resembles what a mature individual experiences upon entering an erotic *temenos*, where the *we* appears as a mutual entity capable of containing my *I* and your *you*.

Unity in a *we* manifests a tripartite structure; for a *we* can only come to presence when a distinct *I* and a distinct *you* have already been established. But for the individual without sufficient self-structure, none of these three elements has been established, and "relationship" is unipartite. Instead, the not-yet-*you* of the "self-object," becomes the lived foundation of an *I* which is still struggling to become. As long as the self-object can be "possessed" and retains adequate stability, the narcissistic individual feels sufficiently grounded to acquire the kinds of experience that will build a sense of having a coherent self of his own.

A lop-sided narcissistic *temenos* is not easy for a therapist to maintain. We find ourselves infected with our patient's emotional chaos as much as he is relieved by our habitual stability. The oscillations of his "unstructured self" from worthlessness and emptiness to "grandiose" power and wisdom are felt in the interpersonal field between us as though they are our own. We become inflated with the conviction that our marvelous self-sufficiency is all that is needed. We will cure him with our transformative love. In this moment we identify with our idealized self-object role for him, and are tempted to believe that some dramatic enactment of our union—perhaps through sexual intercourse—is all that is needed.

But no sooner do we approach this conclusion than the patient himself is infected with the grandiosity afloat in the field between us, and he recoils from union as though it would dissolve what little he has of a sense of self. He reacts with rage, filled with a power that overcompensates for his habitual sense of nothingness. He becomes the wise and sufficient one, and we are plunged into depression and despair.

It requires tremendous determination and struggle to retain a hold on ourselves in such a tumultuous emotional field. What seems to be incipient union reveals itself as narcissistic entanglement. The coherent sense of self we generally take for granted is tossed like flotsam in an emotional surf, and there is little we can do but be aware of this fact, allowing the breakers to close over our head in the confidence that we will eventually bob back to the surface.

Our self-object consistency is precarious at best, manifest primarily through our tolerance and flexibility in the midst of primitive psychic forces. The most we can hope for is that trust in our self's own autonomous capacity for coherence will hold the two of us and establish the possibility of a therapeutic interchange that will "structure" the not-yet-self of our patient and bring us both some measure of peace.

Persisting in the self-object/nascent-self field already expresses a kind of love, for our patient's experience of such relationships has no doubt been extensive and universally disappointing. Because the tumult is so hard to bear, he has been deserted time and again. If we can share this dyad with relative equanimity, we have already taken him more seriously than anyone has. The real work of therapy, however, requires the much more deliberate effort Kohut calls "empathy." We "feel our way in" to the lifeworld of the not-yet-self and "mirror" back what we find—emptiness, grandiosity, rage, longing, etc.—and frame these elements as intimations of his self-to-be.

Empathy is an active form of love; for love, wherever it may be found, sees and affirms the unique reality of the other, is drawn to it and values it. No gushing pretension, no perfunctory praise, no hollow compliment, no fobbing off, empathy takes the other seriously, sees the implicit but nevertheless lived reality of his not-yet-self and expresses it accurately.

As months and years of empathy by a consistent self-object pass, the evanescent self-in-becoming is not only grounded and anchored but explicated in detail. A chaotic jumble of emotions, memories, and fantasies is sorted out, and its elements find their place in the growing coherence of a personality that is finding its center.

In a narcissistic field, "feeling our way in"—which is the literal meaning of "empathy"—is not strictly accurate if we imagine two separate beings, one of whom is psychically "entering" the private space of the other in order to feel what he feels. For the erotic energy of the field is already brimming with emotions that derive from both and influence both. To "feel our way in," therefore, means to feel the mutual passion as a reciprocal condition, to allow ourselves to be immersed in it and to appreciate that it is both of ours. In the midst of this "mystical participation," however, what distinguishes "empathy" from "sympathy" ("feeling in" from "feeling with") is that empathy requires we not lose touch with our own standpoint, our distinctive *I-ness*.

It is as though we have one foot inside the tumult of the *temenos* and one foot outside, firmly planted in our own subjectivity. Awash in mutual feeling realities, we observe ourselves as recipients of the waves of emotion that toss us, recognizing as well as we can how we are contributing to the field, and using our intuition and powers of deduction to construct for ourselves what our patient must be feeling. What we can gather from his words, gestures, facial expressions, dreams, and the like also belong to the picture that emerges.

This work of seeing our patient and then finding a way to articulate what we perceive makes considerable claims upon us as persons. To hold a "mirror" up to him so that he can begin to see himself means that we ourselves have to *be* that mirror. Our affects are reactions to him, as his are responses to us. In the moment we feel all-powerful and selected by fate to cure him with our benevolence, empathy requires us to attain some distance from our inflation and perceive that he is "idealizing" us the same way *we* are. His impotence is overwhelming both of us. When we fail to grasp the nature of the forces that would sweep us away, we are no less a fragment of driftwood than he is. We could stay forever in this emotional whirlpool, learning nothing of our patient and keeping him in ignorance of himself.

Progress, the "structuring of a self," occurs only when we can name these forces: label them, first, so that we can find ourselves, and then discern our patient as our partner. He has been the victim of these forces all his life. The erotic field between us, understood as the interaction of a self-object with a nascent self, gives us living acquaintance of the world he inhabits twenty-four hours a day. Unable to sort it out and find himself as a centered subject, he is simply battered this way and that by the currents. He is grateful that we are willing to share it with him, but he needs more.

We love him by taking him seriously enough to go through it with him, to value him as a worthy partner in Eros. But he has been longing for a love that will find *him* amidst the tumult and elucidate his experience as *his own*, as proceeding from the self he has yet to find. This is "mirroring," because it assembles the images and intimations he fleetingly has of himself as they swirl and tumble between and through us both. It is slow, painstaking work, for he has so little of self to collect them around.

No therapist can hope to meet a patient's needs flawlessly. It is inevitable that our "mirroring" will fail again and again in its accuracy. For it involves no little guesswork, and the mirror that is ourselves is always distorted by our own complexes and self-delusions. We can only hope that our mistakes at the beginning of the work will be few enough and sufficiently inessential that a solid trusting rapport can develop.

As we become better acquainted with our patient and the distinctive *temenos* we share with him, our failures in empathy become progressively more noticeable as exceptions. The more clearly the patient recognizes them, the more painful they are. Each one confirms his worst fear, that he will always be misunderstood, found unworthy, and abandoned.

As our patient reacts with rage, depression, or withdrawal, the stormy field between us intensifies in hostility and confusion. We ourselves feel guilty, self-righteous, and maligned. We are tempted to defend ourselves or to take some "high road" based on our presumed superior wisdom and assert the rightness of our injuring interpretation even more emphatically. These are persona-restoring strategies designed to repair the damage done to our own idealized self-image, and they desert our patient in the moment of his distress. They exacerbate the empathic failure and endanger the self-object/nascent-self rapport that undergirds our work.

In this moment, our patient feels supremely unloved. We have "frustrated" his need to be seen accurately and feelingly, and the only remedy is to regain our capacity to see him lucidly for who he is right now in his desolation and abandonment. No doubt we have slipped off our gratifying perch as the divinely gifted perfect mother and been demonized as a heartless monster. It is humiliating to accept that in the *temenos* of our common work we are indeed a bad and destructive mother.

Paradoxically, however, such errors provide the greatest opportunity, for our patient is familiar with mutual joy when things are going well. What sticks in his craw is the way things go so disastrously downhill the moment he is misunderstood, leading to isolation and abandonment. No one has taken him seriously enough and loved him sufficiently to stay with him when things are going badly. All his life people have dismissed his feelings of rejection and loss with platitudes and hollow consolations.

These moments of disconnection that escalate so inevitably into blame and hostility lie at the heart of his alienation, confirming time and again he is a non-person, unworthy of human community. His touchiness on the subject makes it difficult for us to respond. But our task is essentially no different at this moment than at any other. We must comprehend his emerging self with accurate empathy, feeling his desolation, ratifying his sense that he has been misunderstood, and indeed by us.

In *How Does Analysis Cure?* (1984) Kohut makes it unmistakably clear that in his view what "structures a self" is "optimal frustration." Each time the patient's need for gratification is frustrated *empathically* ("optimally") a large stone has been laid in the foundation of his emerging self. In order to have a self that "coheres" in the face of desolation, he needs a "mirror" to reflect that hardest-to-hold center, the one that is breaking up in consequence of a fractured connection. For us to *be* that mirror, we have to stay in this most difficult *temenos* and hold our own guilt and sense of inadequacy humbly together with his terror, rage, and resentment.

No one has loved him this way before, and no love convinces him more effectively that he remains an almost-self even when shattered by disappointment and misunderstanding. Our sorrow and remorse for what we have done to our patient's self-in-becoming "optimizes" our mistake, retrieves it from the "outer world" of impersonal and arbitrary persona expectations and brings it back into the erotic *temenos*.

Possibly more difficult to handle even than failures of empathy, are demands from the patient that we gratify his narcissistic needs by joining him outside the therapeutic *temenos* by being his friend or lover or by intervening with his boss or his wife for him. Here limits must be set to his grandiosity. But these cannot be restrictions derived from some book of rules or the public world's ethical preoccupations.[2]

---

[2] Though they may hardly be expected to contradict them very seriously.

As empathic, "optimal frustration" looks to the self-in-becoming of the patient, which we behold caringly, fathoming the puzzle of his not-yet-coherent wholeness. Seeing with our heart as well as our mind, we discern the incompatibility between the self-in-becoming and the demand he has placed. We perceive how intensely he desires it, how painful it will be to relinquish, how shattering to be refused. Our "no" is not hackneyed or formal but flows from the sorrow of our heart. In the self-object/nascent-self field, the incompatibility is a self-evident but sad and disappointing fact.

In Kohut's view, "optimal frustration" is so much the essence of *any* genuine analysis, that Freud himself was an inchoate self psychologist—beginning with his legendary self-analysis, the first "depth-psychological comprehension of the total personality" (Kohut, 1985, p. 182). The same kind of "re-visioning" may be applied to Jung's *nekeyia,* his carefully observed and interpreted brush with psychosis.

Furthermore, Jung's insistence that subsequent dreams will criticize mistaken interpretations of prior dreams amounts to a kind of "optimal frustration" theory. Dream interpretation is no impersonal decoding of mysterious messages from an alien unconscious; it is a reading and empathic elucidation of the self of the dreamer by a partner with whom he shares an erotic *temenos.* Misinterpretations are failures in empathy. Their "optimal" handling presumes a caring interpersonal field, where the therapist takes every development seriously as a manifestation of the patient's emerging self. In the last analysis Jung's doctrine of subsequent correction can be understood only in the context of the "love cure."

Self psychology clarifies a crucial issue about Eros and therapy. Freud's statement, *essentially the cure is effected by love,* is open to misunderstanding insofar as "love" is taken to mean a simple impulse toward union, as though sexual intercourse were its ultimate aim. Because we have little trouble rejecting this conclusion as counter to the goals of therapy, we may be inclined to take *effected by love* as a muddled and dangerous overstatement. Kohut's highly refined description of love untangles the confusion. It distinguishes two elements in the erotic field. The first of these is union, the bond between self-object and nascent self that undergirds all therapy. Here, union is not the *goal* of therapeutic love but its erotic foundation and life-giving spirit.

The first intimation of a goal emerges when we consider empathy, which in a certain sense is the opposite of union. For empathy introduces a kind of *distance* into the self-self connection. In order to "feel our way in" to the patient's lifeworld and articulate its emotional complexity, we have to retain our own distinct standpoint as critical observer. Without the self-self bonding of the therapeutic *temenos*, empathy cannot arise; but without the distance of careful observation and clear elucidation, empathy cannot build structure.

Ordinarily we think of love as essentially unitive. We think of mothers hugging their children, of friends delighting in one another's companionship, of lovers' intercourse, perhaps even of mystics who strive to find words for a "Union without Distinction" they enjoy with God. We also carry about a contrasting set of unidimensional images: the blindness of lovers, the loss of individuality experienced in "fusion," the obsessiveness of the infatuated, and the muddled notion of "co-dependency."

Kohut's explication of empathy, however, implies that every occasion of effective love involves both union and distance, because nothing less can affirm the full reality of our partner and desire his well-being. The paradigmatic instances of mature love, ecstatic sexual union and mysticism, might seem to be exceptions. But even the mystics who speak so highly of "Rapture" and "Union without Distinction" admit that their ecstasy is always momentary. They move in and out of rapturous union; and although they experience it as its own reward and seek it as an end in itself, their *distance* from God is a primary concern, if intensely painful. John of the Cross calls it "the dark night of the soul" and credits it with transforming the mystic from a novice to a "contemplative." It is the "refining fire" God uses to frustrate the mystic in an optimal manner.

We have only touched upon the issue of mature love and have not considered a therapeutic *temenos* shared by two reasonably well-structured selves. Still we can understand with confidence how it is that therapists since Freud have so frequently been close to acknowledging that *the cure is effected by love*. As dangerous as this position may seem to be when its implications have not been thought through, it is inevitable. For *the love they have longed for as children* is a serious and passionate clear-eyed regard, whose articulation "structures" their "self."

Erotic union constitutes the means of the love cure, as the ground and life of the work. The distance-amid-union that Kohut calls "empathy" explicates the elements of therapeutic love—if not human love in general. The goal of therapeutic love (at least for those who are still longing for the love they missed as children) is the establishment of a coherent and reliable self.

Five

The Love Cure Part II:

If No Bond of Love Exists,
They Have No Soul

Although Freud applied psychoanalysis almost exclusively to "neurotic" individuals and was suspicious of Jung's attempts to analyze schizophrenics and similarly decompensated patients, many psychoanalysts, following Melanie Klein, have looked to the most primitive of psychic mechanisms as fundamental to understanding human psychology in general. The object-relations school of psychoanalysis has concerned itself primarily with the study of earliest infancy, well prior to the development of an "Oedipus complex," in order to comprehend the functioning of patients who seem incapable of relating to other people as independent, autonomous subjects. Not surprisingly, they have developed models of therapeutic interaction in which the analyst understands her work as supplying the benefits of "good enough" parenting.

In doing so, they have taken up and differentiated Freud's remark to Jung that *essentially the cure is effected by love* and another to Ferenczi that *one could effect far more with one's patients if one gave them enough of the love which they had longed for as children.* This has been no woolly-minded undertaking, but a sober investigation not only of their most severely afflicted patients but of themselves; for each has discovered the truth of Jung's observation that *the person of the doctor is claimed by the work.*

The most recent in this chain of seminal theorists, Heinz Kohut, has explicated the notion of the "love cure" in elegant detail. Essentially he has shown that a lop-sided bond of love between the incoherent and unreliable self-in-becoming of the patient and the relatively stable and coherent self of the therapist ("self-object") establishes an interpersonal field in which the patient's self can be "structured." The work of building a self is accomplished by the therapist's accurate "mirroring" of the patient's nascent self, and particularly by her "empathic frustrations" of his unrealistic demands for "gratification."

Kohut has, in effect, distinguished two moments in the love that effects the cure. The first is unitive, the self-object/nascent-self rapport; and the other introduces a kind of distance, the "feeling in" of an empathy that simultaneously retains its own subjective standpoint. In the first, an unbidden state of loving relation, an erotic *temenos*, emerges as the ground and life of the work. In the second, an active and deliberate course of loving attention strives to attain the goal of a structured self.

Kohut's "self psychology" has therefore clarified and justified what is meant by the recurring theme of the love cure in the many schools of psychotherapy that have developed since Freud revolutionized our thinking. But he leaves us with a problem. Does the love cure apply only to those "narcissistic" individuals whose inadequate parents left them "unstructured," or may it apply more broadly to *any* patient who enters therapy?

Kohut's clinical writings consider only narcissistic patients, and his method is designed to elevate the functioning of individuals who are merely *inchoate* subjects, bringing them to a point where they have sufficient internal coherence to enter human relationships at the most basic level as a definite *I* meeting a unique *you* in the *temenos* of a *we*. He retrieves them from their alienation and introduces them to the human community.

How are we to imagine their progress from this point forward? May they not still require therapy? Has not Kohut emphasized the incomplete nature of the work he reports? Is there any way to apply a self-psychological perspective to patients who are not so unstructured when they encounter us? Perhaps the fundamental question we need to ask is what may an individual *do* with a "structured self." A theory of personality and therapeutics that fails to consider this issue will surely be suspicious. Before we build a foundation, we will want to have a pretty good idea of how the final edifice should look.

Kohut has not ignored this question, although his treatment of it is rather fragmentary. He speaks of relatively high-functioning figures like Goethe, Hamlet, Winston Churchill, and German leaders, like Bonhoeffer, who were able to "maintain themselves" in the face of Nazi-inspired mass regression in the society around them. These are "tragic men," individuals of deep conviction who moved with confidence even unto death *because they followed the program laid down by their nuclear self.* Here is Kohut's "central assertion" on the subject:

> The art of the tragic—whether sung, told, or written as in the great epics; whether through music, on canvas, in stone, or on the stage—is concerned with man's attempt to live out the pattern of his nuclear self. And the tragic hero who is the protagonist of the great tragedies, which must be counted as among the most precious cultural possessions of mankind, is a man who, despite the breakdown of his physical and mental powers (e.g., Oedipus) and even despite his biological death (e.g., Hamlet), is triumphant because his nuclear self achieved an ascendancy which never will, indeed which never can, be undone (Kohut, 1985, p. 37).

Kohut's notion of the self's nuclear program closely resembles Jung's guiding idea, that the self orients an individual along the path of a "personal myth." *Tragic man's* course of "narcissistic fulfillment," her ability to live the deep reality of her nuclear self, frees her from "the fetters of communal living"—although this is apt to inspire a "frightening envious anger" in people insufficiently connected with their nuclear selves.

Because the persona-field atmosphere is so hostile to her "self-expressive initiative and creativeness," *tragic man* will be pressured to "withdraw from her innermost goals and ideals" and find ways to "falsify and dilute them." When she can maintain her mythic course despite the public forces of mass-mindedness arrayed against her, she becomes a hero, strengthened in her course by the harmonious flow of narcissistic energy from her nuclear self. If tragic death should be the outcome of her faithfulness to self, she achieves a fulfillment that can never be taken away. Furthermore, spectators dissatisfied by the restrictive assumptions of public life may come to see her as a model for "the unfolding, expansion, and triumph" of their own nuclear selves. For these people, as for herself, *tragic man's* death is not mourned as a defeat but admired as a narcissistic and timeless achievement.

Whatever we may think of the militant fervor of Kohut's language,[1] his vision of *tragic man* reveals that one's nuclear self continues to be of vital interest even after it has been "structured." She consults and examines it in the form of her "unfolding nuclear program," and uses it to guide her life. We are therefore afforded a picture of an individual who began life as we all did, with an "unstructured" and narcissistic self-in-becoming, and who was fortunate enough to have experienced the right kinds of loving relationships whereby she constructed a reliable and coherent nuclear self. She then proceeds to unfold and live the lifeworld destiny implicit in that self—and indeed more adequately than most people.

Although we know her self grounds and stabilizes her *I*, making her capable of meeting a *you* in the interpersonal field of a *we*, we hear nothing of her relationship life. It would be particularly interesting to know whether the unfolding of her nuclear self takes place primarily in and through loving interchanges with others. We might guess that

---

[1] Such imagery is understandable in a man who fled Vienna for Chicago during the Nazi years and subsequently experienced a great deal of criticism and jealousy from his colleagues in the psychoanalytic community. Because he was born sufficiently late (1913), however, he did not suffer the excommunication of Adler and Jung—even though his doctrine of "narcissistic triumph" closely resembles Adler's notion of "superiority" based on the "as if" of a "life strategy," and his "nuclear program" is very similar to Jung's concepts of "individuation" and "personal myth."

it does, that in the tripartite *temenos* of mature relationship, her *I* is explored and "unfolded" as much as her partner's *you*. If so, this might describe the nature of therapy, friendship, or marriage with an individual who has a vivid sense of living her nuclear self.

If all this is true, as seems reasonable, it would make sense to *extend* the theory of self psychology to deal with interpersonal and therapeutic meetings between normal and even superior individuals. This could be done without changing the nature of self-psychology's description of relationship. Its ground and life would be found in an erotic self-self *temenos* explored through an empathy, which would still be assigned a two-fold task. The first would be achieved entirely within the *temenos* of the *we*, as the patient's lifeworld is caringly examined through attention to the emotions and fantasies generated by her coherent self.

If this resembles "mirroring" in its attention to the germ of the patient's identity, empathy's second function in the field of *we-ness* would resemble "optimal frustration." It would concern itself with the successes and failures of the patient's attempt to live her life's project. Such attempts would take place for the most part outside the therapeutic field in the world at large, where the expectations of the persona field hold sway. There she would be expected to experience a variety of "narcissistic triumphs" and set-backs, the reports of which she would bring back to the *temenos* she shares with her therapist to be evaluated and understood empathically for their lifeworld implications.

It is surely surprising that a psychologist like Kohut who places interaction in the self field at the center of his theory of therapeutics has so little to say about *tragic man's* relationship life. This is particularly puzzling when we consider the nature of an "unfolding nuclear program," for it describes two opposing kinds of relatedness that guide *tragic man*. On the one hand, she has to negotiate a persona field with its inauthentic rules and expectations, while on the other she has to remain faithful to the "narcissistic energies" that belong to the nature of the "self" and "harmonize" them. When she ignores or compromises with the demands of her nuclear self in order to accommodate herself to the pressures of the persona world, she experiences regret, remorse, and shame. She becomes *guilty man*, subject to the "drive conflict" dynamics that Freud elaborated.

Guilty man would be relieved of the demands of her nuclear self in order to relax into an identification with some social role, enjoy acceptance by her peers, and take comfort from an approved path along the main stream of the public world. The inauthenticity of such a course is proven by the grotesque demands of a social ethos such as that of Nazi Germany, although it is to be found in any persona field whatsoever. The antidote to such a neurotic life style is given by the "narcissistic energies" that a nuclear self "harmonizes."

Thus in self psychology, the term *narcissistic* has a dual valuation. On the one hand, it denotes an individual whose self is insufficiently "structured" and is therefore pulled this way and that by fragmentary and unharmonized impulses and overwhelming emotions. On the other hand, "narcissistic energies" are the stuff of a deeply satisfying and creative life course.

Kohut has, in fact, articulated a theory of the psyche that very closely resembles Jung's, where "individuation" is a life course that hews a path between two opposed collectivities, that of the persona field and that of the archetypes. Like "narcissistic energies," the archetypes manifest as impulses of overwhelming emotional power that characterize "schizophrenia,"[2] when fragmented and unharmonized by a "self." But when they are integrated, they provide a depth of meaning and satisfaction, described as living one's "personal myth." It is no accident, in fact, that when Kohut makes his "central assertion" about *tragic man* he refers specifically to mythic narratives: *the great epics . . . which must be counted among the most precious cultural possessions of mankind.*

Not unlike Kohut's description of *tragic man*, Jung's first reference to the mythic possibilities of the "collective unconscious" takes heroic form. In *Symbols of Transformation* (Jung, 1912/52), the sun hero derives his transcendental significance from his kinship with the dy-

---

[2] Jung's notion of *schizophrenia* was much broader than ours is today and included what we presently label *narcissistic* and *borderline* conditions.

ing, rising luminary of the sky, reigning gloriously during the day and dissolving into the womb of the sea every night to fight the demons of darkness and arise renewed. Even twenty years later, in the 1930s,[3] Jung's accounts of individuation downplay the role of the erotic self-self field of therapy to speak almost exclusively of intrapsychic dynamics in the patient: the dream series of Wolfgang Pauli, detailed in *Psychology and Alchemy* (Jung, 1944/52), and the series of paintings produced by a woman in "A Study in the Process of Individuation." (Jung, 1934/50). Only in the late 1940s does he finally address the interpersonal dimension of unfolding a personal myth in *The Psychology of the Transference* (Jung, 1946), where he says, *If no bond of love exists, they have no soul,* and *Wholeness is a combination of I and You* (par. 454).

Although access to Jung's message in *The Psychology of the Transference* is made difficult by the form of the writing (a commentary on a series of alchemical woodcuts), he actually supplies what we are looking for, an account of how the love cure continues to be the means by which therapy achieves its aims, even for individuals who have already developed a "structured self."

In fact it has become generally accepted in recent decades that the experiences Jung describes in this work of central importance derive from his formative analyses with Sabina Spielrein and Toni Wolff, if not also his own brush with psychosis in which Toni Wolff became *his* analyst. *The Psychology of the Transference* is therefore undoubtedly an autobiographical work in which the potentially embarrassing details and their implications are hidden behind the generalized and recondite imagery of alchemy.

In the opening scene, "The Fountain," archetypal energy is "stirred up" to the point that the alchemical author, Christian Rosenkreutz, has the grandiose "realization that he is related to 'royalty'" (Jung, 1946, par. 407). A circular flow of narcissistic/archetypal energy that fertilizes the conscious attitude, kills it, and brings it to life again, has begun its work.

[3] The first versions of these papers were published in the *Eranos Jahrbücher* for 1933 and 1936.

The royalty of the patient meets that of the therapist in the next scene, as king and queen are invigorated by a common grandiosity, and clasp one another by their "affective" and "dubious" left hands. The Holy Ghost of decision, purpose, and divinely inspired movement hovers above, while the serpent of sex, anger, fear, and hatred (unchanneled narcissistic energy) enters from below. A dangerous but promising unitive process has begun.

In the third picture, they are naked: "affinity in the form of a 'loving' approach" carries them forward (par. 451).

In the fourth, they are immersed in a bath, "presumably the sexual libido which engulfs the pair" (par. 455). At this stage in the development of self-self union that characterizes every erotic *temenos*, Jung comments, *If no bond of love exists, they have no soul* (par. 454).

"Soul" is the theme of the whole book. It is the "link" between the Holy Ghost and the serpent of narcissistic chaos that makes possible a coherent integration of our highest unitive aspirations with our lowest instinctual feelings; and it is the ground of genuine relationship.

> Thus the underlying idea of the psyche proves to be a half bodily, half spiritual substance, an *anima media natura*, as the alchemists call it, an hermaphroditic being capable of uniting the opposites, but who is *never complete in the individual unless related to another individual*. The unrelated human being lacks wholeness, for he can achieve wholeness only through soul, and the soul cannot exist without its other side, which is always found in a "You." *Wholeness is a combination of I and You*, and these show themselves to be parts of a transcendent unity whose nature can only be grasped symbolically . . . (par. 454; italics added to the two English phrases.)

Love is the emotional attention by which we take one another seriously and bring soul to presence between us. Soul is not a "substance," as the alchemists believed, but the essence of relatedness itself, the greater reality in which my *I* and your *you* meet, find one another, and discover their reciprocity. The soul that comes into being when we are bound in love is our *we-ness*, the third partner within every erotic *temenos*. It alone makes us whole.

Thus Jung, in no uncertain language, affirms the nature of the love cure as essential also in those therapeutic interactions in which the patient is capable of being both an *I* and a *you*. Possessed of a "structured self" like the author Rosenkreutz, her potential for a greater wholeness and a more satisfying creativity manifests in the image of the fountain, with its flow of archetypal/narcissistic energy—which is dangerous insofar as it threatens the self-synthesis she has enjoyed up to this point in her life, but which offers a new and more complete sense of self-hood. She cannot realize this on her own as an isolated individual but seeks it in the only place it can be found, in the soul that comes to presence when she engages lovingly with her therapist.

Her state of narcissistic or archetypal arousal brings her "royalty," her "grandiose" potential, into the therapeutic *temenos* as symptom of her need for renewal. The infectiousness of her stirred up energy engages our latent grandiosity and brings it to the fore so that we find her not only fascinating, but engaging at the deepest level. Her self and our self, the king and queen of the pictures, are the primary participants in this erotic field. Both of us feel that our meeting is fateful and that something is required of us that cannot be ignored. We embrace it—left hands joined—despite its danger, no doubt feeling that we may as well choose the death of our living soul as reject this "call" which our partner embodies.

If we begin our meetings, as we always do, ensconced in our roles as therapist and patient (suggested by the royal clothing of the figures in the woodcut), the "loving approach" that alone brings soul to presence between us cannot tolerate the maintenance of these personas. We shed them, so as to meet in the nakedness preferred by all lovers, in the truthfulness of self encountering self. Love is not satisfied with outward appearance, but desires to penetrate to the center, to leave nothing concealed, to know and be known in untrammeled intimacy.

Immersion in the bath suggests a deepening "mystical participation," the moment when the soul of our *we-ness* has so much advanced to the foreground of our attention that our *I* and her *you* begin to fade into the background. Jung does not flinch from identifying the water of the bath with "sexual libido" or from admitting that therapist and patient find themselves "engulfed" by a desire for genital union.

In the present-day state of our persona world, we can hardly dismiss this reality as "merely symbolic"; for it is a preoccupation that affects us all. Genital union is unthinkingly assumed to be the goal of all unitive impulses by the public world outside our therapeutic *temenos*; and we who move into and out of these *temenoi* several times a day as part of our profession, know from experience that fantasies of genital union are frequently present. Our task is to find some way to accede to the dissolution without succumbing to literal enactment.

At this point in our therapeutic process, literal sexual union risks disrupting the wholeness that soul makes possible, the "link" between body and spirit. If we ignore the spiritual implications of our impulse toward union in order to enjoy sexual congress, body may overwhelm spirit, the serpent of narcissistic fragmentation may devour the dove of the Holy Ghost. If we are overcome by the bodily instincts of sexuality, we endanger the fading but nevertheless essential reality of our *I-ness* in order to possess our patient's otherness—not as a genuine *you* but as a set of qualities we wish to annex to ourselves. We risk obliterating both our *I* and her *you*. If we lose them, we lose both the *we* that joins us and the soul our mutual loving attention has brought to presence between us.

In the image of dissolution implied by the bath, the *bond of love whereby they have soul* has a dual function. On the one hand, the affective bond expresses the unitive moment of "mystical participation." This is love in its passive, emotional, accepting mode. We allow our love to dissolve our separateness as we enter more fully into our *we-ness*. But on the other hand, the soul that love brings to presence cannot exist without the opposites it joins, body and spirit.

In this sense love requires us to maintain a distance amid our union, a distance that retains our *I-ness* and her *you-ness*, a distance that holds in view the unitive spirituality of the Holy Ghost as well as the fragmentary but fecundating potentials of the narcissistic serpent. "Mystical participation" in "soul" is therefore an active and deliberate kind of loving, a holding of the tension, a waiting for guidance. Our guide in this process is soul, the third partner our loving brings to presence.

The fifth picture in the series, "The Conjunction," shows the king and queen, still naked except for their crowns, copulating in the sea—or in a variant, winged and copulating in the sky. "Union on a biological level is a symbol of the *unio oppositorum* at its highest" (par. 461). Because "things cannot be forced" (par. 464), Jung insists we must co-operate with this unconscious bond while struggling not to lose our therapeutic observer's stance.

In the sixth scene, a two-headed hermaphrodite wearing a single, double-sized crown is lying in a coffin. "When the opposites unite, all energy ceases: there is no more flow" (par. 467). The soul is in "great distress," for absorption of too much narcissistic energy has led to "psychic oedema" and dissociation.

Copulation and death: despite our best conscious intentions, our *I* and our patient's *you* are substantially dissolved into the *we*. Even as we try consciously to maintain the distance that keeps "soul" and its constituents in sight, we are moved by overwhelming forces of affinity and joined in what the mystics call a "Union without Distinction" which nearly extinguishes our *I* and *you*. It is all we can do to remember our role as therapist, struggling to retain a therapeutic standpoint even as we have *become* the process.

The water of commingling is virtually all that is left, just as it is for the mystic lost in the darkness of divine Oneness, whose vague memory of the *process* of achieving union is all he has during that ecstatic moment to remind him of his former subjectivity. Movement ceases insofar as the opposites of *I* and *you*, body and spirit, dove and serpent, enter as fully as we can imagine into an unconscious oneness. Nearly complete loss of subjectivity leaves us depressed and feeling dead.

Jung makes it clear this is not a literal sexual union, but a copulation all the same, in which our two beings have interpenetrated, dissolved, and lost their habitual identities. This ecstatic moment for which we have so greatly longed is almost unbearable, for it brings the death of everything we have known about ourselves. Both "soul" and the love that brings it to presence are in danger. It seems as though the serpent of narcissistic fragmentation has come out victorious. In submitting to the process of loving union, we have sacrificed everything we have held dear about ourselves.

This is why the love cure is so distressing and why it claims the person of the therapist so totally. We give our very selves up to the process and are devoured, hardly able to cling any longer to the fiction that this process is for the sake of the patient alone. We ourselves are in over our heads. We feel the ecstasy and the desolation no less keenly than our patient. Because this is the death without which renewal cannot come to be, we will no longer be the same therapist or the same person we used to be. Our oneness with our patient has achieved a lasting—if not disastrous—outcome.

Still consciousness is not completely vanquished; for depressed and leaden though we may be, there is much work to be done. Jung speaks of dream interpretation and the elucidation of feelings and fantasies that do not cease despite our state of unconsciousness. Because we are so equally part and parcel of this dead-centered lethargy, the temptation to relinquish our fingertip hold on the observing and commenting consciousness that has made us a therapist seems more than we can bear. Why not just admit our ignorance and equality with the patient? Would that not be the most honest course? Has she not brought us to this pass through her unique gifts and the power of her unconscious potential? How do we dare to pose as a guide when we have been so humbly reduced?

Very likely the experience of "conjunction" takes place as the high point of a single session that we perceive as the goal of everything that has preceded for weeks and months. It is a rapturous moment in which we feel transported out of ourselves. Meeting our patient wholly and without reservation in the luminous globe of the *we*, our ecstasy is filled with transcendent meaning, a culmination of the many fantasies of union we have harbored regarding all the erotic partners of our lives. This is the moment we have sought, and it is glorious beyond our loftiest hopes.

Because we have resisted literal, bodily enactment, our union also includes spiritual congress, so that the session very likely ends in silence and reverence before a portentous feeling that its significance will never be exhausted. We have the greatest expectations that from here on out nothing will be the same. Our rapturous course is blazing new trails in therapy and human relatedness. We can hardly wait for our next meeting.

But our next session is dead, depressed, and hopeless. All movement has ceased. Indeed, there may be weeks of this lethargy and puzzling lack of interest. If our patient brings dreams and reports of day-to-day experiences outside the *temenos* of our therapeutic interaction, she does so without conviction. They seem to have no meaning and reinforce the deadness that has overcome us both. If we can rise to the task of interpreting them, we do so only against the greatest resistance. Our own lack of conviction may be the clearest indication that something has gone seriously wrong.

To the extent we can recall the requirements of our therapeutic task and our idealized self-image as a guide in the landscape of the soul, we feel defeated and guilty. There can be no doubt we have been pulled into this death by forces greater than those of consciousness, but the fact that we let ourselves so naively in for it calls into question our very aptitude for our profession. The temptation to give up and admit failure is nearly insuperable.

Despite all indications to the contrary, however, the process has not reached its end. The series of alchemical woodcuts goes on. In the seventh, the soul leaves the coffined body of the hermaphrodite as a small, sad homunculus and ascends into the clouds. This is the dark state of disorientation, when ego consciousness has dissolved and "latent psychoses may become acute" (par. 476).

In the eighth scene, "Purification," the two-headed hermaphrodite in its coffin is drenched in a cleansing dew falling from the clouds. Jung identifies this with "the removal of superfluities" in which discriminative consciousness returns and the idea contained in the dream is "worked through."

In the ninth stage, the soul returns as the same homunculus, diving head-first from the clouds and looking substantially happier and more lively than at departure. Finally there is a light at the end of the tunnel. The soul of loving union restores the possibility of relationship and effective consciousness, for "a radical understanding of this kind is impossible without a human partner" (par. 503).

Hope and the return of a lively interest in the work is surely not immediate, for the stillness of death is succeeded by yet another deadly image: loss of soul. Soul is the link that binds us with loving affection and makes of our *I* and *you* a compelling *we*. It is the very secret and motive force of our common work. Its loss forces us from our stagnation but leaves us open to the unchanneled narcissistic energies that characterize an "unstructured self." The archetypes break loose from their self-synthesis, precipitating a psychotic-like state.

Deadly stillness is replaced by the most terrifying movement. Jung describes this in terms of the *patient's* "soullessness." *She* is "driven willy-nilly without a sense of direction . . . exposed to the full force of auto-erotic affects and fantasies" (par. 476). We can only wonder about his frankness on this point, for in the absence of soul the therapist, too, must face the danger of being "out of control."

Surely in this soulless state, we, too, are at the nadir of our competence. This is the most difficult stage of the work, and requires "the greatest patience, courage and faith on the part of both doctor and patient" (par. 476). The tension of consciousness has been lost, and both of us feel overwhelmingly our powerlessness. Loss of soul diminishes our sense of *we-ness*, even as we both flounder in an unstructured dissolution. Rage and mutual accusations are readily available to provide an inauthentic escape from our intense pain. For is it not *you* who brought me to this pass, and have you not dissolved me into your madness?

Here is where love in the sense of a lucid seeing and articulation is indispensable, the empathy that Kohut has so beautifully described. But at the point that soul is no longer brought to presence by the loving attention of an *I* and a *you*, an empathic stance is nearly impossible to attain. Instead, we can only cling to our remembered identity as therapist with "faith," as Jung insists, clinging to our habitual conviction (however precariously) that these symptoms are symbolic and have a meaning.

Perhaps the best way to do so is to remind ourselves as well as our patient that these events we are undergoing are worthy of study. Very likely we both need to write them down, string them together, and try our best to recall how we may have experienced similar things in the past. "Nobody who ever had any wits is in danger of losing them in the process, though there are people who never knew till then what their wits are for" (par. 479).

When we persist in such an effort despite the strongest temptation to give up, the stage of "Purification" follows with a wonderful alleviation of our dullness and stupidity. No doubt we are still lost and struggling, but now we begin to catch glimmers of meanings we can accept. We erect hypotheses to guide ourselves and collect evidence to confirm and criticize them.

The alchemists, Jung points out, warn against book learning. At this stage of the work, our psychological texts "must be avoided or destroyed 'lest our hearts be rent asunder'" (par. 486). Hypotheses based solely on the intellect and intuition are bound to fail. Heart is required. The dew that falls from the clouds onto the moribund hermaphrodite consists of the feelings without which ideas are empty and dead. Feeling alone distinguishes the "water of wisdom" from abstract knowledge.

A great deal of psychological work must be done during the stage of "Purification," and it resembles most closely the work of empathy as Kohut applies it to the unstructured self of narcissism. For at this juncture in the work toward "individuation" when the soul is still absent despite our ability to work, neither we nor our patient is fully an *I* or a *you*, and our *we* is still lacking. We are bound in a union characterized by narcissistic chaos, when the archetypes are not yet structured by coherent selves.

What is required, therefore, is a kind of anticipation of loving relatedness, where our re-emergent selves are attended to with feeling-filled hypotheses. Jung calls it "the differentiation of ego from unconscious," by which he evidently means discerning nascent coherence amid the flux of narcissistic energies. It is "the necessary condition for the return of the soul to the body" (par. 504).

Relationship in the full sense of the term, as an encounter between an *I* and a *you* in a *we*, is possible again only with the return of the soul; for soul "is the very essence of relationship" (par. 504). The soul re-enters the *hermaphrodite*, the composite being that represents our union with the patient, reconstituting it as a living whole that is no longer disintegrating in narcissistic "putrefaction."

Now finally, the danger and overwhelming confusion is behind us, and we realize that "the *conjunctio* is a *hierosgamos* of the gods and no mere love affair between mortals" (par. 500). We ourselves are not our union; the unique identities of our *I* and *you* re-emerge from our entanglement and the *we* comes again to presence as the Third. A true loving relationship is again possible between a pair of transformed individuals.

We have prepared the ground for the soul's return by diligent and feeling-oriented attention to our nascent coherence during the stage of "Purification." But we cannot be said to have *caused* the soul's return. We experience this development as an "act of grace" not unlike that more dangerous development we enjoyed as "conjunction." The stages of this psychological alchemy are beyond our conscious control. We are limited to persistence, co-operation, and the struggle to prevent our becoming lost.

Our efforts to respond to soul and live with soul have taken us through the darkest night, when soul's absence is the most palpable reality between us. If there is any guide to follow in this blackness, it is John of the Cross' *Dark Night of the Soul*, where he speaks of acceptance and quiet, of learning soul's true reality by relinquishing our habitual means of consoling ourselves. Soul returns only when our attitude has changed, the most transformative function of "optimal frustration." Applied to therapy, we have to accept that we are nearly as much a neophyte as our patient in this work.

The final woodcut depicts the two-headed hermaphrodite alive, winged, and standing on the moon. Jung emphasizes the monstrous nature of the alchemical goal: "I have never come across the hermaphrodite as a personification of the goal, but more as a symbol of the initial state . . ." (par. 535).

The end is not the end, but only the beginning. The alchemists identify it as the "new being," the "son of the philosophers" or the "philosophical stone." Something has, indeed, been accomplished. The *we* between therapist and patient is renewed and transformed. We have a vision of what is possible, but more work needs to be done— very possibly involving new conjunctions, new deaths, and new restorations.

Unfolding a personal myth or nuclear program is never achieved once and for all but requires intensive work, patience, and constant repetition. The living hermaphrodite is a vivid personification of the commingling and lack of differentiation that persists, even after the greatest advances have been made. Soul is present between us as the unique reality our loving attention, through its many vicissitudes, has made possible. What has been "unfolded" in this work is still "monstrous," and remains an inadequate guide along the path of individuation.

The fact that Jung ends his account of *The Psychology of the Transference* at this "initial state," speaks of life's ceaseless process, wherein goals recede and change as we approach them. The patient has begun her process dissatisfied with her life's course and with her narcissistic energy stirring. This generates a mutual situation in which *our* latent grandiosity and need for personal renewal is intensely engaged. We approach one another with loving attention, each feeling completed by the other, as soul in the form of a *we* is brought to presence. Soul draws us into conjunction, death, and terrifying confusion before re-emerging as the living hermaphrodite. When it does re-emerge, however, soul has a distinctive character all its own which sets the agenda for our continuing work.

Soul appears at the beginning of our work as a boundless and unspecified possibility. We experience it primarily as a draw into union, with little notion of what to expect of this pull, knowing only that it is numinous and irresistible. It leads to a lengthy and painful entanglement. When the dust settles and our *I* again faces her *you*, we find ourselves in a soul with features—monstrous perhaps, but redolent of what we have given to our relationship. Soul manifests not emptily, as before, but full of what needs to be unfolded.

Furthermore, the coherence of our selves has changed. The old, outmoded syntheses have been replaced. Having structured these selves mutually, we know them intimately, and have come to trust their autonomous capacity to dissolve and reform. Each of us is more secure in a synthesis that has revealed this resilience. As we begin our work again from this new "initial state," we do so with more sobriety, more awareness of what we are letting ourselves in for, and a better indication of where we are going.

Individuation "unfolds," we may conclude, through a series of these hermaphroditic monsters, each a synthesis of new narcissistic energies and each a call to further engagement through love and soul. Soul draws us out of our isolation and completes us in stages. Each step of the way requires a new utilization of *empathy*, the active love which recognizes, clarifies, and articulates a self that moves from coherence through dissolution in a *we* into new coherent and resilient syntheses.

Individuation only *begins* once a coherent self has been reliably established through a love cure characterized by the lop-sided union of self-object and nascent self. Individuation *proceeds* by way of a love cure rooted in a relatively balanced self-self bond that brings soul to presence. From this point onward, soul is our guide, dissolving our respective self-syntheses and leading us from one preliminary vision of our goal to another. The ground and life of this work is the unbidden unitive love that establishes a self-self bond. The means is the active and deliberate *empathic* love that accepts what it cannot control but discerns and ratifies emergent possibilities. The goal is the unfolding of a new personal myth—not only for the patient but for ourselves as well.

The implications of such a vision do not restrict the development of soul to the arena of psychotherapy. As the alchemists believed they were only applying the forces of nature to speed up nature, so Jung sees therapy. It is an *opus contra naturam* because it deliberately imitates nature in order to outdo nature's slow and uncertain course. The natural force that accomplishes the work is love. Love, wherever it brings soul to presence and is attentive to soul, unfolds self, leaving us more adequate to *be* ourselves, to *become* ourselves, and to negotiate the world.

The great lovers of human history—people like Teresa of Avila and John of the Cross in Christianity, Jelaluddin Rumi in Islam, and the *bhaktis* of Hinduism—were never able to flee the practical considerations of the public world in order to rest in some narcissistic, unchallenging, and isolated *temenos* of union. They were the founders and administrators of religious communities who had to struggle with day-to-day affairs as well as with their political and theological critics. They were powerful, integrated personalities who had harnessed their "narcissistic energies" to achieve a superior mode of existence.

No doubt they established a code of rules for their religious orders, but we can hardly imagine them as narcissistically grandiose and fragmented in their dealings with their companions and novices. They must have loved them empathically, recognizing and responding to the *we* emerging in their meetings, with all the union and distinction that this implies. Superior individuals of this type—although they all had "spiritual directors" with whom they shared the lives of their souls—had no theory of psychotherapy by which to unfold the personal myth they so obviously lived. They allowed *soul* to teach them what we have learned from the several schools of psychoanalysis.

Six

Therapy and Sex

Both in structuring a self and unfolding a personal myth, the love cure takes place within and illustrates the *structure of erotic interaction*. There is a unitive moment in which our *I* and *you* feel drawn into a oneness that would dissolve our former identities into a greater whole. Whether our longing to merge into the *we* is greeted with joy and hope or fled in terror and despair, it inevitably meets its opposite, the distancing moment. For union's promise of what we might become is always opposed by our fear of losing what we have had. However paltry and incoherent our sense of self may be, it is the only identity we have known; and the prospect of giving it up means ceasing to be as we have been: ceasing to be our "selves."

As Kohut and Jung have shown, the dissolution of unity threatens us with narcissistic formlessness, the chaos of unchanneled archetypal energies, that would break us like a slick of crude petroleum on a turbulent sea. We are faced with existential dread, the threat of nothingness, the death of ourselves. But even as we flee it, we are brought up short; for we have glimpsed possibilities that render our habitual self-synthesis a narrow imprisonment. We can no longer go on as we once did, and yet we dare not submit.

Every erotic *temenos* is characterized by this oppositional pull, such that if we are not to go on vacillating forever, we must either flee the field, or resolutely hold the tension. "Empathy" is the name Kohut has given for "holding the tension." With his articulation of the multifaceted meaning of empathy, he has uncovered the *structure of erotic interaction* as the foundation of therapy. Empathy requires that we stand *in* our union while at the same time refusing to relinquish the *outsider-hood* of our subjectivity. For only the *outsider* has sufficient *I-ness* to see what is going on and keep it conscious, and only unity's *insider* maintains the process itself. Without unity's *inside*, its loosening and rearrangement through "melting" and interpenetration, there is no process. Without the *outsider-hood* of a distinct and observant *I* and *you*, there is no one to "mirror" and "frustrate."

Jung's *leitmotiv* (*If no bond of love exists, they have no soul*) describes the erotic *temenos* in condensed form. "They" are *insiders* within the bond of love; yet only as the plural *they*, standing *outside* one another and facing one another, can "soul" come to presence between them. Therapy strives for and exploits the tripartite structure of erotic interaction, wherein a distinct *I* and *you* contemplate and love one another through the transcendent reality of their *we-ness*. This distance-amid-union characterizes every erotic interaction: without union it would fly apart, without distance it would collapse.

Erotic tension might also be described as the *two faces of unity*. On the one hand, unity promises enlargement, completion, wholeness, and transformation. This is what Jung ascribes to the dove of the Holy Ghost hovering above the king and queen in the alchemical woodcuts, the bringer of spirituality, transcendence, and divinity. On the other hand, unity threatens us with chaos, fragmentation, and annihilation—the mercurial serpent of narcissism that enters from below to leave us unbounded, unstructured, and incoherent, flotsam in the waves of primal emotion.

We have taken as our guide, however, seminal texts from several Christian mystics that seem to have known only one face of unity. For them, God is goodness itself, unalloyed with any evil, and they suffer solely by being separated from their divine Lover. Can they have known only the dove? Or do they simply fail to speak of the face of destruction?

There is no question that the Yahweh of the Pentateuch is a God of terror. No one can look upon that Face and live. Yahweh must be near his people, but not too near. Such duality is furthermore not confined to the ancient Hebrews. For if John the Evangelist is the same John of Patmos who wrote the Apocalypse (Book of Revelation), as Christian tradition insists, the God of Love is also a God of Fear.

The history of mysticism is not unaware of this ambiguity. Many of the contributors to the Jewish Kaballah tradition report terrifying encounters with the God they pursue. Jung wrote frequently of the Swiss Catholic saint, Br. Klaus, who had a shattering encounter with God and was only able to hold himself together by studying theological texts and painting his vision on the wall of a church. By placing orthodoxy between himself and his vision, he was able to regain the distance his *I-ness* required. If a great deal of what he had seen was lost in the dogmatic form he finally assembled, he must have felt well rid of it. For too much of God, too much of divine unity, would have destroyed his human subjectivity. He would have been devoured by the serpent of narcissistic incoherence.

Martin Buber, whose mature writings are filled with invective against mystical union, hints at the reason for this in one of his earliest books, *Daniel: Dialogues on Realization* (1965). The character Reinold tells the following story:

> This spring on my journey home out of the south I came one evening to Spezia. I had wanted to travel on throughout the night, but the sight of the sea was so powerful that it foolishly struck me to want it despite my intention. I descended, went to the harbor, took a small boat and rowed out. It was a new moon, but from the depths above me a chorus of southern stars sang down upon me; my oar cut dark flood and concealed splendor; boundlessness was the bed of my soul, heaven, night, and sea its cushion. It was one of the hours in which we no longer know more strongly what we do than what is done about us and with us. So as I now turned the boat and returned to the shore I was barely conscious of the action of my hands.

Now I looked up casually—and was terrified. Everything that I had just now possessed had disappeared. Out of a dumb infinity an army of jack-o'-lanterns stared into empty infinity; threateningly, thousands of moist lips, sneering cruelly, opened and closed about me, and in the nape of my neck, dark and tangible as a betrayal, the presence of the night beings grew. Where the bed of my soul had been, was the nothing; seduced, betrayed, rejected, my soul hung in the gray of the night between sea and heaven. I did not understand, but I steeled myself for battle: "I am there, I am there," I cried, "and you cannot annihilate me," and strength spurted into my shoulders and my legs at the same time, and gripped, with the feet firmly planted and the oars out: to the shore!

Then a shrill conflict of light swept over a piece of the shore and tore it loose. . . . (pp. 84f).

If the terrors of a loss of *I-ness* experienced by the Patriarchs of Judaism, the Kaballists, John of Patmos, Br. Klaus, and Buber's Reinold, belong to the unitive moment of mysticism, as we can hardly doubt they do, we must conclude that the great mystics had to have been possessed of a superior self-synthesis. Either they had an extraordinarily coherent subjectivity to maintain their *outsider-hood* in the face the overwhelming *we* they shared with God, or God was uncharacteristically gentle with them.

The unitive moment alone effects no benevolent transformation. It must always be accompanied by distance. For this reason we have had to conclude that erotic union can not be the *goal* of therapy, even though it is its ground and life. The goal is to be sought first in the structuring of a self and later in the unfolding of a personal myth. These are accomplished by the distance-amid-union that Kohut calls "empathy."

Insofar as our concern all along has been to understand how it is that therapy is so frequently threatened by impulses to sexual enactment, we are relieved to discover that its goal is distinct from the unitive pull of Eros—for it is union that we associate with sexuality. Earlier we found some comfort in discovering that erotic interaction has a structure all its own that need not imply sexual enactment— even though the unthinking attitude of our contemporary persona field confuses "the erotic" with "the sexual" at every turn. Our every-day language perpetuates this muddle, in that to call a gesture, a mode of dress, or the tone of a movie "erotic" is generally to mean "loaded with sexual allusions."

Still, our relief at finding that therapy's goal is not simply unitive is, in all honesty, premature. It arises from the argument of Chapter Three, in which the unitive dimension of erotic interaction was explored in terms of the testimony of the great Christian mystics concerning their unity with God. We found that their experience had a great deal of relevance for the unitive dimension of therapy. Not being able to exclude the unitive impulse of sexuality from this picture, we came dangerously close to approving of sexual activity as a tool to enhance erotic union—even in the domain of therapy. Our fear of being found in conflict with the "fundamentalism" of the persona field (*any aspect of sex in the context of therapy is always wrong*) caused us no little anxi-ety; and we placed all our hopes in a distinction we had not yet explored. Although Eros was surely the ground and life of therapy, perhaps it was not identical with therapy's goal.

We clung to the hope that an investigation of therapy as the "love cure" would uncover a "goal" distinct from unity; and our hope has been partially justified. We have determined that the goal of therapy is two-fold, the structuring of a self and the unfolding of a personal myth, activities that require distance between the *I* and the *you*. We might even imagine—though we have barely touched upon this pos-sibility—that the goal of therapy is *fully* realized when the patient is able to continue the unfolding of his personal myth after terminating the therapy itself. Perhaps we are not required to justify this assump-tion further, in that therapy always takes itself to be an *episode* in a patient's life, an opportunity to straighten oneself out, to discover one's own proper identity and how to live it.

Surely this is implied in the concept of unfolding one's life program—if this unfolding is, as it must be, a project that lasts as long as life itself. Jung emphasizes this point in calling therapy an *opus contra naturam*. Therapy is a process which exploits the forces of (erotic) nature to assist the natural unfolding of a life that has mired itself in "neurotic" and "unnatural" hang-ups. He frequently states that the goal of analysis is to make the patient self-sufficient in carrying on a life-long dialogue with his emergent wholeness.[1]

Because therapy as love cure requires *two* kinds of distance (that which belongs to the nature of empathy and that which requires termination), we might hope that sexual enactment in therapy is surely excluded in all its forms. But to rest content with this conclusion would be to ignore two issues that have been fundamental in our discussion. The first is that, even in its goal, therapy remains erotic. For empathy, as "distance-amid-union," belongs to *structure of erotic interaction* even as it establishes therapy's goal.

The second issue has never been examined but only assumed from the outset, namely that sexual interaction is one modality among many within the domain of Eros. Therefore, if sex is a kind of erotic interchange and therapy is erotic from start to finish, we now find ourselves in a more embarrassing position than we did before investigating the nature of the love cure. We have established no definitive grounds for excluding sex from the therapeutic *temenos*.

Let us try to formulate our problem more precisely. We have found that the love cure employs the *structure of erotic interaction* for therapeutic purposes. Furthermore, it describes the essence of the therapeutic endeavor itself. This is so much the case that every effective therapy, whether it understands itself this way or not, is at bottom a love cure. But because "the erotic" is difficult to distinguish from "the sexual," acknowledgment of the erotic nature of the love cure

---

[1] For example: "I am persuaded that the true end of analysis is reached when the patient has gained an adequate knowledge of the methods by which he can maintain contact with the unconscious, and has acquired a psychological understanding sufficient for him to discern the direction of his life-line at the moment." (Jung, 1916, par. 501).

raises the alarming possibility that sexual activity may seem implicitly to be approved. We are anxious that we may fall afoul of the persona field's prohibition of sex in the therapeutic *temenos*.

Our problem arises precisely here. We find ourselves torn between the requirements of a nuclear self and those of the persona field. For, as love cure, therapy structures and unfolds a self. It imposes no rules from the outside. Indeed, Kohut's sketch of *tragic man* insists that the inauthenticity of a life lived in conflict with one's "nuclear program" arises from attempts to compromise the requirements of one's nuclear self in order to conform to the pressures of the persona world. Jung makes a similar argument in defining "individuation" as a course which avoids dissolution in either collectivity: that of the persona field and that of the archetypes.

This means that to employ the arguments of the persona world for excluding sex from therapy would amount to nothing less than the very compromise the love cure sets itself against. It would be to undermine the premises of our work. We need to frame our question about sex in therapy in a manner that respects the nature of the love cure. We need to know if there is, in fact, anything in the nature of therapy, as the structuring and unfolding of a self, that excludes all forms of sexual involvement.

Once we have stated our problem this way, it is clear that two categories of sexual activity can never belong to the love cure because they do not belong to the *structure of erotic interaction*. The first was illustrated in Chapter Three, when we considered the advertisement for telephone sex from the *hot and horny sex-starved nympho*. We determined there would be no opportunity for an *I*, a *you*, or a *we* to come to presence. Surely this and every form of sex that falls outside the tripartite structure of an erotic *temenos* excludes itself *a priori* from the love cure.

The second category of "the sexual" which conflicts by its very nature with the love cure is *lust*. For as was discussed in Chapter One, lust aims to collapse the tension of the erotic field by denying *distance*. This eliminates the possibility of empathy (distance-amid-union) and prevents therapy from reaching its goal.

In both cases, sexual activity strives single-mindedly for union. If we could establish that it is in the nature of sex to deny the distancing moment in erotic interaction, we could be satisfied that any form of "the sexual" within a therapeutic context would in principle be a corruption of the love cure; and we could argue with confidence that the persona field's absolute proscription is fully justified—albeit for reasons no one until now has been willing to put forward publicly. But is it true that "the sexual" is intrinsically unitive and hostile to all forms of distance?

When we consider the very image of sexual intercourse, the penetration of one body by another, the intermingling of bodily fluids, and the like, it does seem as though sex aims solely at union. A large number of psychological concomitants of physical union also point in the same direction: e.g., imaginal bodily sensations of openings dilating in the abdomen or breast and the feeling that we have entered one another even before our bodies have touched. Sex surely amplifies the sense of dissolving and interpenetration that belongs to the unitive moment of Eros. Bodily union seems to literalize and anchor the psychological pull toward oneness we feel in any erotic interaction.

Furthermore, if the prospect of intercourse is not pull enough, the kisses and caresses of foreplay surely heighten it. We may feel our partner's fingers on our bare arm or waist as electrically tantalizing; and even our own fingers on her cheek or thigh may bring waves of anticipatory melting, dilation, and straining toward union throughout our own body. We feel ourselves opened and prepared. A river runs through us that may rage torrentially when we touch or are caressed in the erotogenic zones. The pull to oneness becomes overwhelming, and we can hardly doubt sex aims at union.

Perhaps all these activities are performed and experienced behind closed eyelids. When we open them, the experience changes appreciably. As we gaze into our partner's eyes while caressing, kissing, and even copulating, still further barriers seem to fall. It seems as though we see into one another's soul. We have never been so open before, so intermingled.

Something else happens, too, when we gaze into our partner's open and undefended eyes. We are struck as never before by the absolute otherness of her independent subjectivity. Our *two-ness* comes to presence incontrovertibly. We find ourselves engaged in a union-across-distance. We are aware of our *I-ness* and her *you-ness* as irreducible components of our oneness.

Experiences such as these confirm our original assumption, that sex participates fully in the tripartite structure of an erotic field. Distance is by no means foreign to it. If we try to speak while making love, distance reasserts itself so strongly as to compromise and deaden the tantalizing pull toward copulation. But if we speak of our mutuality in this moment, we return to our union-amid-distance as soon as we again fall silent. Indeed, our union may be enhanced both by what we have shared and by the reminder our speaking brings us of the insuperable *two-ness* our union seeks to dissolve.

Over the course of weeks and years, we accumulate experiences both *inside* and *outside* the *we*. Perhaps we carry the awareness of our shared *we* into our separate activities in our professions and our dealings with the public world, never losing a sense of our unique separateness but conscious nevertheless that the *I* we have become has been interpenetrated and enlarged by the oneness we share by night. On the other hand, the *I* we bring back to the sexual *temenos* of our partnership is expanded and differentiated by our individual lives *outside* our union. Our union grows as we do, nourished both by our love-making and our lives outside the bodily exploration of our *we*.

Clearly, then, sex may participate in every aspect of erotic interaction. A sexual relationship, indeed, even calls for empathy—for our having sufficient distance to see, appreciate, and affirm our partner's unique identity and to be with him in the difficult moments. In recognizing and embracing one another's self-hood, we "mirror" each other; and in suffering with one another's pain—particularly in the pain we ourselves cause—we "optimize" moments of misunderstanding, injury, and agonizing separateness. Thus empathy, in its two-fold nature, belongs to the structure of sexual interaction. A sexual partnership that is fully erotic may be the most important *temenos* outside of therapy by which nuclear life-projects are discovered and unfolded. Fully understood and fully lived, sex shares many of its most important aspects with therapy.

Given this picture of sexual interaction as thoroughly erotic, our difficulty in excluding sexual enactment from the love cure has grown immeasurably. These two domains share the same structure and may even accomplish the same goals. We are confronted with the possibility that the love cure may have no intrinsic grounds for excluding sexual activity. Perhaps the persona field has intuited this possibility in the absolutism of its extrinsic demand: *no form of sex is ever permissible in therapy.*

But let us not give up so easily. Perhaps if we take the love cure apart and consider its elements one-by-one, we will be able to establish the inappropriateness of sexual enactment at each stage—albeit for different reasons each time.

Let us begin with the moment of dissolution wherein the love cure opens us both, therapist and patient, to the dangerous but transformative effects of narcissistic/archetypal energies. When Jung says of the image of the alchemical bath, *presumably the sexual libido engulfs the pair* (1946, par. 455), he points to what is surely the most widely feared manifestation of sexuality, its potential to overwhelm and fragment consciousness.

This is sexuality as instinctual insistence, one of the factors comprising the chaotic maelstrom Kohut calls "unchanneled narcissistic energy." It has the power to dissolve the coherence of our self-synthesis, leaving us "obsessed" and "compulsively acting out." There can be little doubt that special attention to this destructive force drives the persona field to make an absolute of its prohibition of *any aspect of sex* in therapy. Under the right set of circumstances, none of us is invulnerable to its corrosive effects upon our conscious will power. Indeed, it is precisely our need to limit the damage such a sexual drive can do to our integrity, that we need a "structured self."

This primal impulse toward sexual union may not even deserve the name *lust*; for lust at least requires the intimation of a distinct *you* and an overwhelming *we*, and acts to obliterate them by making the emergent *you* "mine." Lust implies a modicum of *I-ness*. But the sex drive, as a competing element in the narcissistic/archetypal maelstrom of an un-structured or de-structured[2] self, cares nothing for ego or the niceties of social interaction. It would impel us to repeated acts of intercourse with a single partner, or with anyone we can find. Its insatiability would not stop short of rape or other cruelties, so that our floundering sense of self may grasp at any perversion or inhibition in hopes of setting limits or managing its unfettered insistence.

Freud has called this chaotic body-centered manifestation of sexuality the "polymorphous perversity" that is natural to earliest infancy. Jung identifies it with the mercurial serpent of ego-dissolution. Kohut locates it within the chaos of "unchanneled narcissistic energies." Clearly it is the dark face of union. Its opposite manifestation, the light face, is wholly spiritual but equally inadequate to a well-functioning life.

Pierre Janet, in his two-volume work, *De l'angoisse à l'extase* (1926) describes a case in which the "dove of the Holy Ghost" accomplished no little confusion. His patient, Madeleine, had been an "ecstatic" from the age of eleven, took a vow of chastity and fasting at twelve, and left her upper-middle-class home at eighteen to follow a life of vagrancy, poverty, and Christian witness in the slums of Paris. Her state of "ecstasy" was marked by insensitivity to outward stimuli while she was enjoying glorious visions and a sexual relationship with God which she experienced as orgasmic, although Janet observed her masturbating during some of them. The meaning of the Trinity was revealed to her, and she believed she was capable of levitating, a sign from God that she should float from Paris to Rome to demonstrate to the pope that the bodily Assumption of Mary into heaven was not only a physical possibility but should be declared a Catholic dogma.[3] What she believed to be levitation was clinically observed to be an intermittent hysterical[4] rigidity in the muscles of the feet, legs, thighs, and abdomen, that forced her to walk on the balls of her feet.

[2] I.e., a formerly structured self that has dissolved in the face of unchanneled narcissistic energies.
[3] This was some forty years before a later pope actually did so.
[4] Janet believed there was also a neurological component to this phenomenon, syringomyelia. The diagnosis could only be confirmed by autopsy, which was never performed.

The dark face of union was not foreign to her experience, either, for she also suffered intense periods of sexual guilt and believed herself responsible for crimes against France, in which she was an agent of the devil. There were also periods painfully devoid of union in which she lost all belief, feeling empty and impotent.

Elsewhere I have shown that Janet's work with her was a kind of "soul making," the structuring of a self, which eventually enabled her to leave the Salpêtrière asylum and return to her saintly work in the Paris slums. (Haule, 1984). The reason for mentioning Madeleine in this context, however, is to demonstrate how an unintegrated sexuality may manifest in a highly spiritual manner and lead to experiences very similar to those enjoyed by the great mystics, even in the absence of a coherent self-synthesis. Thus, what Jung calls the dove of the Holy Ghost, the purely spiritual manifestation of erotic sexuality, may be as destructive as the narcissistic serpent.

Whether overly spiritual, as in the case of Madeleine, or simply instinctual, these manifestations of dissociated sexuality belong to the "raw material" of an erotic interaction—the disconnected elements that Eros stirs up when a potential *I* meets a potential *you*. They may be the elements of an erotic dissolution in a *we* or the swirling chaos that prevents their victim from recognizing any other person as a distinct *you*. As symptoms of an unstructured self, they indicate that a balanced erotic *temenos* is not yet possible. Union in a genuine *we* will require prodigious work.

These archetypal emotions and impulses are "pre-erotic" and may, in their most fragmented form, preclude the possibility of any therapy at all. In the lop-sided *temenos* of the therapy of narcissism, they require containment by a structured self. Therapy aims not to augment them but to integrate them into the wholeness of a self.

Surely any form of enactment of the sexual element within the primal flood of narcissistic energies would be counter to the central thrust of therapeutic work. We may confidently conclude, therefore, that *therapy with an unstructured self precludes every form of sexual enactment*. For the essence of structuring a self requires that the therapist see and affirm the emerging self of the patient.

Furthermore, recognition and response to any single impulse that happens to be overwhelming the patient in a given moment—whether this be sexual or not—can only be "empathic" to the extent it recognizes the potential self-hood that is inchoate and implicit in the experience of being overwhelmed. Sexual enactment with a patient whose self-synthesis is still incoherent would amount to seizing upon and augmenting the energy of the sexual instinct above the drowning wholeness. Favoring chaos over structure, it would have precisely the opposite effect of therapy's goal.

This conclusion limits our problem with sexuality to the later stage of the love cure, when its goal is the unfolding of a personal myth and the patient has a relatively coherent self. We assume that this more stable individual is less likely to be hurt, but note with some discomfort that the maxim "as long as no one gets hurt" has been the rallying cry of the sexual revolution of the 1960s, where "casual sex" was championed as an enjoyable and enriching experience.

Our understanding of an unstructured self suggests that "casual sex" in the context of therapy will always be a hurtful experience, insofar as it risks throwing the narcissistic maelstrom even further out of balance. "Casual sex" can only be benign between relatively coherent selves. Superficially considered, this might seem to imply that "casual sex" between a therapist and patient with a structured self cannot be excluded from the therapeutic *temenos*. But first we need to ask ourselves whether "casual sex" belongs to the *structure of erotic interaction*—however "enjoyable and enriching" it may promise to be.

In ordinary parlance, "casual sex" refers to single adventures, "one night stands," at one end of the spectrum, and to relatively long-lasting alliances between individual who may refer to one another as "fuck buddies" on the other. The "casualness" of such alliances refers to the partners' determination not to "get involved." We can well imagine that some sense of *we-ness* may be included in some of these liaisons, thereby making them tripartite erotic encounters.

But while self-hood is the central concern of the love cure (and its pursuit claims the total personality of the therapist) the self-self union that might lead me to contemplate a casual sexual experimentation would itself be relegated to secondary importance. My primary interest would be to prevent my life from being "unduly" affected. In such a case, my partner is largely reduced to the role of a "sexual object" to assist me in adventure or orgasmic release. She never becomes fully a *you* who is interesting for me as the unique individual she is; and our *we-ness* is deliberately banished to the margins of our encounter. We invite one another to bed in the same spirit that we would choose a good movie on video-tape or sample *hors d'oeuvres*.

Peter Rutter (1989, pp. 140-142) reports a story about a psychiatrist he calls Dr. Noren who kept office hours from 3 P.M. to midnight and often spent the night in his office instead of returning to his family in the suburbs. The woman, ex-patient, who related the destructive effects of her affair with Dr. Noren to Rutter felt she was his "star patient" until he abruptly broke it off and asked her "to go back to being just his patient again." She had no doubt another woman had supplanted her, although he refused to talk about it. She was asked to "get over it" and deal with it rationally. "He believed you could think your way out of anything."

Clearly there was nothing to justify even the most distorted notion of "optimal frustration" in his handling of his female patients. He had set up his practice as a kind of sexual smorgasbord for his own delectation. This is "casual sex" in the guise of therapy, and bears no resemblance to the love cure. His partner was, at most, barely a *you* for him, and he evidently showed no attention to her unfolding self.

This consideration of "casual sex" enables us to sharpen our guiding question. The essential issue is not whether sexual enactment may be benign in the sense that it may do no irreparable damage to the patient. Casual risk of damage as an arbitrary factor is always excluded from a therapeutic *temenos*. We wish to know whether sexual enactment can ever *belong* to the love cure as a full participant in the structure of therapeutic interaction. If so, the full erotic potential of sex would have to be used.

This means that the identity and unfolding complexity of the patient's self would have to be served by sexual activity *no less effec-*

tively than by forswearing sexual embodiment of the distance-amid-union which is the essence of the love cure. Only then could we say that sex cannot be eliminated as a valid procedure within therapy.

At this point in our investigation, we have excluded all forms of sex from the therapeutic *temenos* except those that enact the tripartite structure of erotic interaction. By its very definition, this limits the question about sex to the more advanced stage of the love cure, when a structured self is being unfolded. We wish to know whether there is any way to exclude this highly developed form of sex from therapy with a structured self. It is not an easy question to answer. Perhaps we can approach it by considering an even more intriguing story from Peter Rutter's book (1989, pp. 66-70).

A psychiatrist identified as Jim Francis relates a therapeutic sexual transgression of his own—evidently his first and only. His account makes it clear that he understands the issue of erotic attraction in purely persona-field terms: "the magic of having sex with a patient" struggling with his fear of "losing control" and endangering his reputation and his marriage.

He had been "flooded with sexual fantasies" about his patient, Leah, long before the day she asked for a hug after "a particularly painful session." Against his better judgment, he complied and felt his sexual arousal begin and grow. Most importantly, he felt she accepted it. He phoned her later, and they had a brief affair. "But nothing lived up to that magical moment of our first embrace." When they both came "to feel how wrong it was," he referred her to another therapist and entered therapy himself.

Jim Francis' account makes it clear that the "magic" of sex lay for him in his being "accepted," sexuality and all; and he believed that this would "heal" him. It seems evident he had caught a whiff of the love cure but had no understanding of Eros. An erotic field came to presence between Jim and Leah, and in their befuddlement they fastened on the sexual tone of their fantasies and tried to live them in a literal manner.

Jim failed to notice the emerging *we* and lusted to possess the healing balm of the "magic." He collapsed the erotic tension, in the delusion that the unitive moment of an erotic interaction could be sufficient in itself. He gave up his *outsider-hood* to dissolve in the bath of unchanneled narcissistic energies, because he felt them invigorating—as indeed they are.

At the outset of the story, he tells Rutter there had been several patients before Leah for whom he had felt so dangerously tempting an attraction that he believed he had avoided sexual enactment only by luck and fervent prayer. We may therefore conclude that his self-synthesis had been fairly incoherent in the realm of the sexual instinct. He had tried to force it into submission with ethical maxims, a purely ego-centered endeavor, the very flotsam narcissistic energies toss on their crests and drag in their undertow.

Surely Jim Francis demonstrated a good deal more integrity and awareness of the erotic than Dr. Noren with his "sexual smorgasbord." But even ten years later, as Jim tells Rutter what he learned of his own "woundedness," he is in flight from acknowledging the erotic nature of the love cure. For although we may grant that the hug, in his words, had "crossed the line," we are intrigued by what might have happened if he had seen this event in the context of the *structure of erotic interaction.*

The "magical" sexual arousal in that hug *was* the "conjunction." He might have known that subsequent sexual adventures—and even therapeutic sessions—would be characterized by the depression and hopelessness of the "ascent of the soul." The "flood" of sexual feelings and fantasies he had been fighting for weeks was evidence of the "bath." But when he lost his *outsider's* stance, the hermaphroditic soul of his relationship with Leah was truly defunct; and distance could only be re-established in the form of separate therapies for each of them.

We might ask if this need always be the case. We can imagine a therapist in Jim Francis' situation whose self-synthesis is not so compromised with respect to sexuality. He, too, would have felt the "bath" of dissolution with its flood of sexual fantasies. But instead of seeing them as an opportunity for his own healing, he would have taken them as a manifestation of "soul," a coming to presence of a "marrying" *we*, a reality which is not simply *mine* but *ours*. Here we are reminded of Harold Searles' testimony reported in Chapter Five, that a successful analysis is generally accompanied by a feeling of being married to the patient.

After the painfully difficult session, when Leah asked for the hug, a much more coherent Jim would have realized its potential to heighten the sexual tension between them; and the nature of the love cure would have obliged him to consider whether her request was a demand for inappropriate gratification requiring "optimal frustration." He would have looked, in short, to the condition of her self-synthesis, and his own. His decision would be made within the context of the unfolding of Leah's life-project.

Such a scenario brings us face-to-face with our dilemma long before the question of intercourse arises, but its implications cover the whole field. May a hug, caress, or even sexual intercourse, *ever* serve the purpose of unfolding a personal myth and therefore be permissible within the context of the love cure? We ask this question in full knowledge that Kohut and Jung, the two psychoanalysts who developed theories of personality and therapeutics within the context of erotic interaction, explicitly and repeatedly rejected any practice that would deliberately intensify the transference and countertransference feelings. We take it for granted they had good reasons for this. But we wish to know whether the structure of therapeutic interaction *itself* forecloses sexual enactment or whether it leaves the question open.

Implicitly we have already answered this question. For, although we have eliminated all but the most highly refined forms of sexuality from the love cure and found that even they will be inappropriate to all stages of therapy that do not involve well-structured selves on the part of both therapist and patient, we have been reduced to considering specific cases. We may well be suspicious that any form of sex in the context of any therapy will be ill-advised and even counter to therapeutic intent. But we have reached the point where we have to admit that the love cure, by its very nature, has to consider sexual enactment as a very dangerous open question.

This places us in great discomfort *vis-à-vis* the persona field with its satisfying certainty. But the unfolding of a nuclear self always brings us into tension with the public world. It belongs to the very nature of a life lived in harmony with self that public maxims, however self-evident and sensible they may seem to be, are always open to question. This does not mean they are to be disregarded. Indeed, Jung constantly asserts that they represent the *consensus gentium*, the distillation of the experience of thousands of individuals over many generations. They express a wisdom that may never be flouted but at the same time may never be taken for granted.

The unfolding of a lifeworld implicit in a self is always an individual project that can leave no premise unexamined. The base line of judgment always resides within the requirements of the nuclear self. The process of individuation is rarely if ever comforted with certainties. It is a life-long experimentation undertaken with deep sobriety and relying on a feel for one's own integrity—a condition that recognizes mistakes will surely be made.

Thus it is not only the successful patient of the love cure who becomes *tragic man*, but first and foremost the therapist. *Tragic man's* relies on a critical but determined attention to the feedback supplied by the sense of satisfaction, creativity, and deep coherent meaningfulness arising from the narcissistic energies channeled by her unfolding self. This may be expected, in Kohut's words, to arouse the envy of individuals who have compromised the unfolding of their selves in order to enjoy a comfortable sense of belonging to an approving public world. The "tragic therapist," therefore, risks envious opprobrium in order to be faithful to the profound nature of the love cure.

Envy is the central word, here, and used advisedly in the sense Melanie Klein has articulated in contrast with *jealousy*. In "jealousy" we want to *be* the object of our emotion, while in "envy" we wish to destroy her. I may be jealous of a successful therapist who has a large number of wealthy patients who are all profiting dramatically from their work while providing their therapist with a financially comfortable life. To say that a denizen of the persona field is "jealous" of the "tragic therapist" who stands by the implications of the love cure even to the point of leaving open the question of sex, would be to imply that he would very much like to leave that question open for himself.

Perhaps he secretly hopes to set up a "sexual smorgasbord" of his own.

No doubt there are such individuals. But *envy* implies something else. The "envious" spokesman of the persona world would attack and destroy the "tragic therapist" because he cannot stand to have anyone occupy such an anxiety-causing position. The very existence of the "tragic therapist" reveals another way of being and another way of doing therapy. It resonates, probably unconsciously, with his own neglected nuclear self and brings to presence the intolerable anxiety of his own inauthenticity. It disturbs his illusory comfort, and he would destroy the reputation of the "tragic therapist" in order to restore his own complaisance. He would close the dreadful question she has deliberately and soberly opened.

While the "tragedy" of *tragic man* resides in her falling afoul of the persona field's determination to shut out the most dreadful questions that arise from the requirements of a nuclear self, we who would articulate and defend the nature of the love cure can hardly afford to take comfort in heroic notions of going it alone and standing firm. We are not excused from ethical considerations but plunged more deeply and problematically into them. Not being able to fall back on absolute maxims, we are required to investigate the ethical requirements of the love cure in fine detail. For if the question of sex in therapy is to be left open in principle, it must be confronted again and again at every turn in every therapeutic encounter we undertake.

We can hardly dare to begin our work as therapists of the love cure without first articulating the parameters that would guide our handling such a dangerous open question. This will be the topic of the next chapter.

Seven

The Ethics of the Love Cure

The absolutism of the persona field's position (*no aspect of sex in the context of therapy is ever justified*) is both understandable and necessary. By its very nature, the persona field lives by maxims and rules that apply to everybody. Because it is evident that therapy is an erotic kind of work and "the erotic" is inevitably confused with "the sexual," temptation to sexual enactment within the context of therapy is an ever-present danger to everyone.

This has become increasingly clear as reports of sexual misbehavior on the part of therapists have become rather common in recent years, and the damage done to their patients is not disputed. Consequently, a large number of individuals and groups (therapists, lawyers, injured patients, and their supporters) have had to become more and more outspoken in order to assert what should be self-evident. Sexual "acting out" in therapy can be very injurious to the patient; it takes place in a contractual relationship where the therapist's power to influence the patient can be immense; and it stems from the "woundedness" of both parties.

In a sexually charged therapeutic atmosphere, it is difficult for either party to remain conscious. Delusions about the meaning of sexual feelings may be rampant. The persona field rightly reacts to such a problematic situation by absolutely forbidding any form of sexuality. Misguided good intentions are ruled out completely, along with destructive opportunism. Neither therapists nor the public may be encouraged to think that it is ever acceptable, and the full force of the law must be expected to enforce it.

Unfortunately, however, public confusion about the meaning of "the erotic" and "the sexual" has led to an impoverished and distorted notion of the nature of therapy. As we have seen in the foregoing chapters, therapy, deeply understood, is always a love cure. It always takes place within and illustrates the *structure of erotic interaction*, whereby an *I* and a *you* meet one another in a *we*. This involves a unitive moment that would dissolve the two independent subjectivities of *I* and *you* and a distancing moment wherein the two individuals retain their *outsiderhood* from the dissolving *we*.

The resulting distance-amid-union aims for the structuring of a coherent self in "narcissistic" individuals who have been incapable of holding their own against the unchanneled archetypal energies of their unconscious. In better functioning individuals, it aims for the unfolding of a nuclear self, enabling them to appreciate the personal myth that provides a sense of deep satisfaction, creativity, and meaningfulness for their lives.

Because the impulse to physical union enacts the *unitive* moment of an erotic interaction, it largely obscures our recognition of the distancing moment. When Eros is lustfully "sexualized," therefore, its nature is distorted, its project prematurely truncated, and its goals remain unreached. Public confusion about Eros and sexuality results from our failure to appreciate the very existence of a distancing moment in an erotic field; and Eros itself is depicted as sexually dangerous.

In reaction to this confused state of affairs, an idealized public image of therapy has been developed, representing it in an unrealistically safe guise, wherein the emergence of a powerful *we* is held to be suspicious. The erotic feelings inherent in every numinous *we* are taken to be evidence that something has gone wrong. Sexuality as a "neurotic" or cynical opportunity looms.

When "the erotic" is confused with "the sexual" in this way, the persona field speaks of "boundaries" and wishes to erect safe barriers. However, we have seen in Chapter Two that "boundary language" employs metaphors that would deny the very *structure of erotic interaction* and subvert the therapeutic process. In this way the persona world's ill-conceived ethics of safety from the dangers of sexuality obscures the very work that therapy is trying to accomplish. Our investigation of the love cure has been an attempt to set the record straight and encourage therapists and patients alike to make clear a distinction between Eros and sexuality. Eros is the ground and life of therapy and—of itself—by no means implies "sexual acting out" or even sexual feelings.

But the problem of ethics in the field of therapy is even more complicated than this. For although the love cure respects the good intentions of the public consensus, its aim of discerning and unfolding a nuclear self inevitably comes into conflict with the collective maxims of the persona world. The "unfolding" or "individuation" process that is therapy's goal gains little support from the persona world's generalities. It is supported, on the contrary, by the individual's unique, personal feelings: the sense of integrity, creativity, and wholeness generated when "narcissistic energies" are channeled into a coherent and meaningful way of life.

It is as though the love cure would have us turn our ear *inward* to stay in tune with ourselves, while the persona field calls to us from the *outside* through the din of the crowd. If the masses are wrong and our integrity is high, we may become *tragic man*. On the other hand, if we deceive ourselves about the tune our self is piping, we may be no more than misguided fools.

The persona field is on the lookout for the fools and the damage they may do. Its broad public consensus, therefore, makes no concession for individual variations and idiosyncrasies. Although one of the sure marks of foolishness is an arbitrary flouting of publicly approved morality, conscientious conflicts between the demands of the self and those of the persona field are inevitable. For the individual's needs can never be totally harmonized with society's generalized expectations. The love cure, therefore, struggles constantly with the pressures of public ideas and values.

For example, our patient may find her personal integrity too much compromised by her job. Her unfolding self seems clearly to indicate she needs to find a new way of life. But simply leaving her profession is not an easy thing to do. In the short run, at least, it will mean a loss in financial well-being and prestige. She has to grapple with her priorities; and we do, too.

In the *temenos* of the love cure, we focus on her emerging sense of self. But we also have empathy for her predicament. We reflect back to her in sorrow our appreciation of her dilemma. Our loving comprehension of her turmoil recognizes both her needs for coherent narcissistic gratification through well-channeled archetypal energies as well as the requirements of everyday life in the "real world," where persona-field conceptions hold sway.

Although we do not *recommend* one solution over another, the very fact that we bring the issue of her self-hood prominently to the center of our mutual concern, *demotes* the absolutes of the persona field. We take them as propositions that may be questioned and examined. Despite Kohut's heroic language, a "nuclear program," when it guides a human life, hews a middle course between the need for inner harmony and the requirements of outer adaptation.

We cannot practice the love cure without running the risk of being seen as "heretics" by defenders of an official truth. Perhaps there are many areas—such as financial success and professional prestige—in which we do not mind being so considered; but when it comes to the question of sex in therapy, we become very uncomfortable indeed. We hate to be out of line in this dangerous sector of the persona field.

But despite our high regard for the wisdoms enshrined in a public consensus shared by millions in the present and across several generations, our work is to champion the neglected self of our patient. Furthermore, we are ourselves individuals engaged in unfolding our own self-synthesis. Consequently, both in our work and in our personal lives, we bear a responsibility soberly to question every proposition: those offered by the persona field and those posed by a developing sense of self.

If we are committed to following a path like this, there ought to be some among us who are willing to spell out the ethical considerations that guide us. Surely the persona world has its articulators and defenders, as indeed it should; for its positions must be shown to be rational and consistent. In contrast, our self-guided ethic may well seem to those who have not explored it, to be an arbitrary and even sly way to claim any license we desire. Because we are the minority, we have, if possible, a greater need for ethical definition. For we have to defend what is not obvious to the majority.

As regards the persona field's absolute prohibition of sexual enactment in therapy, we have already conceded its full applicability to the first stage of therapy (the structuring of a self)—although we may have done so for reasons the public has not considered (the exacerbation of an emerging self's incoherence). Even with regard to therapy's second and final stage (the unfolding of a personal myth), we have ruled out all forms of arbitrary and "casual" sexual experimentation. We have made it clear that the love cure's focus and the justification for its methods reside in a accurately empathic regard for and articulation of the patient's self. What is arbitrary or "casual" with respect to this central principle may distract from or even destroy the work.

We have had to leave open the question of sex only when the following two conditions are met. (a) The therapy is taking place between two relatively coherent selves—and we might add that their coherence extends also into the realm of sexuality. (b) The unfolding of the patient's self seems to call for some kind of sexual enactment, as part of the work itself.

It must also be emphasized that the serious work of individuation may never disregard the wisdom of any public consensus. The maxims of the persona world require serious and sympathetic investigation. Therefore, we will be highly suspicious of any eagerness we might detect in ourselves or in our patient to employ some form of sexual enactment as part of the therapeutic work.

As cautious as we may be, however, we *have* left the question open. We have no choice but to spell out the complicated parameters and procedures that would have to be observed, if we should ever find ourselves having to consider the possibility of including sexual enactment as part of the love cure.

We have often stated our "bottom line," the *structuring and unfolding of a self*. But a great deal is implied in this shorthand expression. Most significantly, there is not one self unfolding in the erotic *temenos* of our interaction, but two. We have devoted all of our attention to the meeting of these two individuals in a *we*. Now it will be necessary to investigate each of these subjectivities, for every therapeutic move will impact both therapist and patient, as well as their *we*. We shall begin with the simplest issue, the notion of sexual enactment as it affects the person of the therapist.

We assume the therapist is a stable individual, who has gained a close acquaintance with the quality of his self's coherence: through his own years as a patient in therapy, through wide experience as a therapist himself, and through a self-critical life-course. The emergence of sexual feelings in his meetings with others—including his patients—is a phenomenon he has observed repeatedly. He has explored these feelings through verbal and bodily interactions with several lovers, and very likely he has been involved in one or several long-lasting sexual partnerships in which he has been exposed to the full range of emotions, conflicts, and intimacy. No doubt the *thought* of sexual enactment with a patient is by no means foreign to him. Nevertheless the caution and skepticism of a healthy engagement with his nuclear self on the one hand, and the persona field on the other, has given him sufficient reason to reject acting upon the thought.

Now for the first time it seems a cogent possibility. His first response is to doubt the coherence of a self-synthesis (his own) that seems to call for such an unorthodox procedure. He is well aware of the persona field's disapproval and of its reasons, but is inclined to believe that *this* course of therapy with *this* unique patient may be an exception. The very inclination, however, is itself a reason to be skeptical. For he is aware that every earnest therapist who has ever fallen in love with a patient believes his own case to be an exception. Indeed, he may actually know other therapists who have been mistaken in this belief, and he has seen their patient/lover casualties in his own practice.

He is familiar with the quality of narcissistic/archetypal energies and how they appear in each case to be uniquely powerful and redolent of truth. Every couple to fall in love believe themselves to be the first people ever to have experienced these transcendent feelings. Such convictions of uniqueness seem thoroughly collective and banal only from the outside. He knows he must become an *outsider* to himself in order to get a confident grip on what is happening to him.

Probably he begins by examining his past, paying particular attention to those relationships in which he eventually uncovered self-delusional thinking, obsessiveness, and other indications that archetypal energies had escaped from his self-synthesis and asserted their own agendas. He will be particularly careful to apply these recollections to the present. To what extent does the current notion of enactment in the context of therapy resemble those past instances of blindness? Is this questionable intention integral to his present self-synthesis, or has it broken loose? To what extent is he fascinated by it? Is it merely an enticement to experiment, or does it seem to be essential to the unfolding of his personal myth?

If he decides in favor of the latter, his attention will be directed toward the future. What fantasies does he have with regard to the sexual involvement he is contemplating? Where does the self's unfolding seem to be taking him? Is he hoping for some kind of personal "healing," only? What kind of enlargement of his being is portended here? Is it really an organic development of the self whose coherence he has come to know through diligent introspection, or is it overloaded with unrealistic fancies of a grandiose nature? Could he articulate these matters to a sympathetic but well-grounded listener, or would he feel foolish? Would these fantasies sound sensible outside the *temenos* he shares with his patient, or do they have to be kept secret?

When he gets to this point in his deliberations, he will surely realize how difficult it is to become an *outsider* to himself. He will be reminded of how easily he can be fooled about his own intentions and the nature of his unfolding self. His abilities to assess the intentions implicit in his nuclear program are always uncertain, and he knows from experience that following the course of individuation is a little like flying an airplane in a storm. One relies on one's instruments to indicate divergence from the course and corrects accordingly.

In less dicey areas, he would surely risk erroneous decisions and gladly pay the consequences; for following a personal myth always involves cautious experimentation and recovery. But in this weighty realm the possibility of deluding himself may involve great dangers—not only as regards social condemnation but particularly because this time the dangers affect another whose psychological health is entrusted to him.

Perhaps his humility in the face of so momentous a decision and the untrustworthiness of his objectivity will lead him to seek help in the form of supervision. If so, he will look for another practitioner of the love cure, a therapist who is aware that the unfolding of a self requires a critical but respectful skepticism regarding the certainties of the public consensus and a similar attitude toward the momentous feelings of transcendent purpose and meaning arising from archetypal energies that may or may not be well channeled.

Our therapist needs a supervisor who will not advise or prescribe but will listen with intelligent objectivity, questioning his assumptions, and probing his unconsciousness, attending to his unfolding self. He seeks a sober investigation of his fallibility and possible inflation, so that his judgments may be rendered more reliable.

The issue of his own individuation project is but the simplest and least dangerous matter confronting him. His role as therapist demands a careful and equally skeptical treatment of his patient's self-synthesis. He will encourage—even insist—that she probe the uncertainties of her own coherence as rigorously as he is doing with his own. They will review together her past, particularly her romantic and sexual history, looking for patterns of self-deception and instances of neediness that have fractured and distorted her self-synthesis.

What motifs may be discerned there, and how do they apply to the present notion of sexual enactment with him? What kind of future is implied in her fantasies? Is she trying to tie him to herself in the hopes of establishing a permanent solution for her dependencies? Is she interested in illicit adventure to grandly declare her independence and heroic identity as against the banality and generality of the persona world? Has her sexual instinct broken free of her self-synthesis to become a dangerous and unreliable factor redolent of what Freud has called "polymorphous perversity?"

Are these energies "channeled," or are they working to dissolve her habitual coherence? If so, what would be served by such a dissolution? Furthermore, his questioning of her past history, present feelings, and future hopes, turns him back to himself, as they supply additional issues for probing the synthesis and unfolding of his own self.

The love cure is defined by its striving for a clear-eyed perception of the other's central, unique, and ever-changing identity—the precondition for empathy. Consequently, a therapist who finds himself in the ticklish situation we are considering will be obliged to pay special attention to the images he harbors concerning his patient's distinctive *you*. He will be required to articulate these (as in every "mirroring") and to pay particular attention to her perception of him.

How accurately does he see her? Is he doing justice to her perception of herself? If she seems flattered or insulted, he must wonder why. Has he seen something she defends against or hopes for unrealistically? What is the meaning of her blindness in this regard? Is he perhaps "projecting," imposing qualities upon her that belong to unexamined narcissistic needs of his own that have escaped his own self-synthesis?

In the same manner he must pay very close attention to the implications of everything she says about him. What sort of agenda may lurk in the images and ideas she reveals? Does he recognize himself in what she "mirrors" to him? Or does she have a distorted, over-valued image of him? He must sharply examine his own reactions, on the look-out for feelings of inflation and anger. For these point in two directions: back to his own self-synthesis and forward to what the accuracy of her perceptions of him say about herself.

If he has sought out a love-cure supervisor to assist in his quest for objectivity, all these matters will be grist for the mill of this secondary *temenos.* What relevance do these transferential and countertransferential images have for his understanding of his own erotic past and hers? What do they reveal about the present condition of his interaction with her? What do they portend for the future? The self is a tricky guide that must always be listened to but never without intelligent skepticism.

Whether or not our conscientious therapist and patient ever get to the point of carrying out the notion of sexual enactment, our investigation has implied two advantages the love cure has over any lesser form of therapy that takes its guidance from an unquestioning reliance upon the absolutes of the persona field.

First of all, the scrutiny we are describing can arise only when certain questions have been left open. Absolute prohibitions close off these questions and prevent our probing areas of unconsciousness by prematurely declaring them off limits. Issues not available for intelligent investigation operate like the "complexes" of the individual psyche, keeping crucial areas of experience and decision completely in the dark.

The love cure employs a daring soberness that aims to leave no pressing area of unconscious intention unexplored. It takes the unfolding of a pair of selves as its central concern and does not flinch from investigating realms the public world deems too dangerous to approach. In doing so, it may appear foolish and of dubious morality from the frightened perspective of the public consensus. But the therapist of the love cure knows this and uses the well-advertised terrors articulated in these broad maxims to sharpen his ever-questioning skepticism.

Secondly, the love cure displays a far greater attention to the uniqueness of its patient's *you.* According to the maxims of the persona field, the patient is always a weak, vulnerable, easily damaged neurotic whose fantasies of sexual involvement with her therapist stem inevitably from her "woundedness" and "lack of boundaries." The therapist is always powerful and overly influential, and the patient a potential victim in an unbalanced power differential. Prematurely closing off these questions reinforces the inequalities, reasserting the illusion of the therapist's infallible wisdom as well as the patient's putative incompetence. In regions like this, where the patient's desires and fantasies are prejudged against absolute maxims, there is little possibility for her to be seen as the structured self she is. She is measured against a rigid stereotypy.

According to the persona field, the patient is never a *you* reliable enough to be trusted with such considerations. She may never be an exception to its preconceived image of what a patient must always be. The love cure, on the contrary, takes the uniqueness of her *you* as the precondition of its work. It leaves every question open, critically and soberly, so as not to prejudge her but to enable her to *be* herself, to *become* herself, and to enlarge her conscious appreciation of the limits and potentials of her unique self-synthesis and nuclear life-course.

To this point our examination of the ethics of the love cure has limited itself to the *I* and *you* of the therapeutic *temenos*. We have detailed the critical issues that arise when these two individuals examine their mutual fantasy of embodied sexuality as it expresses the coherence or lack of coherence of their own separate self-syntheses. We have raised and implied countless questions regarding the tentativeness of every individual's appreciation of a nuclear self known by experience to be reliably coherent but always open to doubt as regards new issues that have not yet been lived but only contemplated. We have adumbrated the multifold nature of our constant uncertainty regarding the self we live as the ground and guiding principle of our lifeworld. We have seen that this can never be adequately explored if questions are prematurely closed by the dogmatism of generalized maxims, however well-intentioned they may be.

To complete our survey of the ethical issues intrinsic to the love cure's refusal to accept the persona field's maxims as absolute, we must consider the central fact of therapy's work, its *mutuality*. In every erotic *temenos* there is not only an *I* and a *you*—each a complicated, unique, and ever-changing self-synthesis contemplated from the fallible perspective of a limited ego. Above all, and most prominently present as a burning reality between us, is the *we*.

The *we* is reducible neither to the *I* nor to the *you*. Furthermore, it is not merely our summation in the sense of the association that consists of the two of us. It is rather a unique reality that partakes of *me* and *you*, but no one else. Every *we* is a unique entity that expresses a mutuality that is "ours."

Although we recognize ourselves in the *we*, it stands over against both of us, rather like a third entity in our meeting. It is uniquely itself, the mutual sum of actualities and possibilities that is our common project, our mutually shared life. It comes to presence between us as the not-me and the not-you that is "ours." Yet even as "ours," it remains mysterious, threatening to dissolve what we have been into its own reality. But if it should ever accomplish this longed-for and dreaded dissolution, it, too, would cease to exist as surely as the *I* and *you* that make it possible.

We mutually contemplate the promise and the threat of our *we-ness* in much the same way and with many of the same feelings with which we separately regard our individual selves. It has the overwhelming power to dissolve us, as do the narcissistic energies that comprise our self; and it has the self's potential for establishing a new transformative synthesis. The *we* is to our separate subjectivities very much analogous to what the self is to our separate egos. Just as each of us relates to our self as the central, partially-known-mostly-unknown agent of our life project, so we relate to our *we* as the recognizable but mysterious agent of our mutual life together.

For these reasons our *we* may be considered the third partner in our relationship. It has its own life, not strictly *separate* from us, but nevertheless different from both of us. It makes demands on us both that may generate conflicts between us or engage us in common endeavors. The love cure itself may be taken as a prime instance. The *we* that is maintained through our tension-holding stance of "distance-amid-union" guides our work, drawing us into activities we might never have considered in its absence. The issue of sexual enactment in therapy is a dramatic example. Does the *we* require this of us, or is it some lustful avoidance of our *we-ness* that drives us to seriously debate such a dubious notion?

The therapist who is considering such a departure from publicly approved behavior is required to bear constantly in mind the fact that the *we* has an agenda of its own that may not be the same as his or his patient's. He must be cognizant of the possibility that the *idea* of sexual enactment may have arisen not as a demand for literal intercourse but as a requirement to follow a certain line of questioning. Perhaps it is the idea and not the execution that is important. It may be that these issues could never arise so forcefully and effectively in any other context than as a literal *possibility* demanding an open-minded inquiry.

In short, it may be the *we's* agenda to engage therapist and patient in a discussion like this that is obviously excluded from the public conception of therapy's role, so that they will define, defend, and alter their respective notions of who they are, individually as selves, and as participants in their unique erotic *temenos*. To take the *we* seriously as the third party and guiding agent in therapy, means to keep an open but critical mind regarding such a question. Is the *we* drawing us toward sexual enactment of our feelings of mutuality; or is it our separate individual proclivities that yearn for sexual expression, while the *we* harbors quite different intentions?

The third stage of intelligent skepticism that comprises the ethics of the love cure has to do with respectful but critical attention to the third partner in the *temenos*. Because we cannot become acquainted with the *we* as agent until we first know ourselves, the ethics of the love cure begins by demanding of therapist and patient a thorough appreciation of their own subjective identities. The love cure therefore requires three separate critical discussions: a dialogue between the ego and self of the therapist, another between the ego and self of the patient, and a "trialogue" between the two individuals and their *we*.

Just as the two dialogues take a respectful but critical stance toward a generally coherent self that may nevertheless have failed to channel the full range of one's narcissistic energies, so the "trialogue" takes a similar stance toward a *we* whose coherent channeling of our individual proclivities is open to intelligent doubt.

149

Our *we* is never wholly in harmony with what we as individuals can agree upon. Perhaps the most obvious illustration of this outside the context of therapy would be an ill-advised marriage that is entered upon with great enthusiasm and hope but ends after a few months in disappointment and rage. We may surmise that two such naive individuals had believed that mutual attraction justified hopes for a lasting and stable companionship. They separately desired to be married and took this as evidence of mutuality. Meanwhile, their goals and expectations for what a marriage should be evidently differed substantially.

They failed to consult the *we* that had come to presence between them in order to determine what *it* wanted. In retrospect we can imagine that the *we*'s agenda was to bring their individual hopes and plans into "trialogue" with their mutuality. Such a "trialogue" conducted with the discipline of distance-amid-union would have revealed a host of discrepancies and left a variety of options. Among these would be a process of individual transformation on either side of the *we* to bring each into harmony with a nuclear self.

A therapist and patient confronted with a lively possibility of sexual enactment would have to engage in a similar "trialogue," asking: what do *I* want, what do *you* want, and what does our *we* want of us. Here is where distance-amid-union finds its fullest expression. When the therapist asks *what do I want*, he means "I" in the sense of his structured self. "You" refers to the self of his patient. "We" refers to what is demanded mutually of the two of them, quite apart from their individual desires.

What the *we* wants of a therapist and patient can be discovered in moments of profound mutuality in which they find themselves sharing the same feelings and entertaining the same images. Examples of such mutuality have been discussed in Chapter Three, where the stages of mystical union provided a structure for understanding the unitive moment in therapy. Such feelings and images are themselves powerfully exciting. Therapist and patient are sure to find them suggestive and overwhelming.

The sense of mystical participation seems confirmatory of the greatest possibility of union in the *we*. But just here, when the infectiousness is at its height, the therapist of the love cure must be on the look-out for deception. The situation is closely analogous to that between an ego and a self when narcissistic energies promise enlargement and an exciting new sense of purposiveness and creativity. The feelings must be both respected and doubted.

In the "trialogue" with his patient and their *we*, the therapist is required by the ethics of the love cure to examine such unitive feelings in several ways. After taking stock of his own reactions, he must ask his patient to describe in some detail what she is experiencing. Any divergence in her feelings and images from his own will suggest an imperfect mutuality. This must be examined. No doubt they share a good deal in common, and this may be attributed to the *we*. But the discrepancies between them are no less telling, for they betray how each of them is responding to the pull of the *we* in different ways.

By means of an extended critical examination of their feelings of mutuality in this way, therapist and patient will begin to discern the three-fold nature of their interchange, as they clearly differentiate his self-synthesis, hers, and the mutual synthesis that is their *we*. If the highly unlikely notion of sexual enactment is ever justified, it will be when it seems clearly demanded by the unfolding of all three of them.

This, however, does not mean that an "affair" is justified. For we have noted that sexual enactment takes many forms. In all probability something as simple as a touch on the arm or a hug would be the first manifestation of sexual embodiment. Therapist and patient are still meeting in a therapeutic *temenos*, and their first physical gesture (as well as any other they decide to carry out) is part of the therapy.

The love cure is always tentative and respectfully critical. Every move in the erotic *temenos* is made and responded to empathically, scrutinized caringly to determine whether and to what extent it manifests the unfolding of a self or a *we*. A sexual gesture made in this context has as great a potential to further or to obstruct an unfolding as does the interpretation of a dream. Mistakes will always be made and sooner or later recognized for what they are, failures of empathy, which require the humble employment of further empathy ("optimal frustration").

According to the persona field, the Dr. Francis of Chapter Six who recognized his mistake in sexualizing the relationship with his patient, Leah, did the right thing in ending their association cleanly and directing the two of them to separate therapies. Under the circumstances this was surely a wise course, for he had no appreciation of the love cure and had made no effort to see the sexual feelings between the two of them as manifestations of an *I*, a *you*, and a *we*. Their hug itself exacerbated unchanneled narcissistic energies that neither of them had sufficient coherence to sustain.

His first mistake was not the hug itself, as a hug, but his abandonment of empathy's distance-amid-union. Without this he lost his capacity to maintain an intelligent skepticism regarding his hopes for a personal healing through sexual embodiment.

The love cure by its very nature always proceeds in a step-by-step fashion, evaluating every move for its adequacy to further the unfolding of two selves and a *we*. It knows that mistakes are not only inevitable but generate valuable evidence regarding the identity of the *I*, the *you*, and the *we*. In general, a sexual error will not be sufficient reason to abruptly terminate the therapy. The empathic process continues as long as the coherence of the three partners is not so thoroughly compromised that "optimal frustration" cannot be employed.

As we have seen in Chapter Five, through our review of Jung's *Psychology of the Transference*, a "conjunction" between the selves of therapist and patient in the "soul" of their *we* lies far short of the goal of the love cure. If their sexual enactment occurs as a "conjunction," powerful but well-channeled narcissistic energies in all three syntheses will provide them a rapturous experience of confirmation. Although this will surely seem a triumph for the triple unfolding that has been the heart of their work, they may expect that their next therapy session (and a large number to follow) will be characterized by deadness and confusion.

This hardly proves their "conjunction" was a mistake. Rather than calling for an abandonment of their work, the "ascent of the soul" only changes the quality of their therapeutic interactions. The task of therapy goes on, despite the fact that its unitive moment has come near to obliterating the possibility of obtaining distance. In a spirit of depression and confusion, they work to understand what has happened to them, to find again an *I* and a *you* that have become lost in a *we*.

The ethics of the love cure is a complicated and heavy responsibility shouldered again and again in every moment of every session. To leave dangerous questions open, therefore, lies at the furthest extreme from irresponsible license—regardless of what the public consensus may assume. Ethical decisions in the context of the love cure are based upon the principle of respectful and critical doubt directed toward the maxims of the persona field on the one hand and the symptoms of an unfolding self on the other. Furthermore, there is not one self but three to attend to, and mistakes are not necessarily evidence of failure but crucial data regarding corrections that need to be made.

Although the therapist bears the primary responsibility in this process, he does not *direct* the therapy like the captain of a ship. We might better liken his work to that of a navigator bending over his charts and instruments, looking for evidence that the vessel of therapy has drifted off course and devising corrections that will bring it back in line with its goal, the unfolding of a self.

The ethical task of the love-cure therapist is short on certainties and long on doubt. Even the metaphor of the ship's navigator is overly precise. For the love cure sets sail on uncharted waters. Every self and every *we* is unique, a new sea with new islands and new continents. The persona field imagines clear sea lanes between New York and London. The therapist of the love cure is as foolish as Columbus.

Eight

Marrying the Patient

While "sexual acting out" in therapy is universally condemned, relatively permanent and committed relationships between people who have terminated a course of therapy with one another have not generated a solid public consensus. In their divergence, the ethics codes adopted by a variety of therapists' professional associations reflect this confusion. Some absolutely forbid any form of social contact at any time. Others set more lenient limits whereby social encounters must be scrupulously avoided for two, three, or five years after termination. As a society, we are clearly doubtful about friendships and marriages between individuals who have had a therapist/patient relationship. But we are reluctant to forbid them utterly.

Probably our lenience stems from our respect for committed partnerships. Few therapists are unacquainted with couples who began their association in therapy. Those I know have been married for years, even decades, and by all appearances have established mature and satisfying alliances. Although I have never heard anyone argue that these marriages should not have been made, the couples live under a kind of cloud. The therapeutic origin of their marriage is never mentioned, and generally the only people who know of it are old friends who can be trusted to keep silent.

Clearly, public toleration even of committed alliances is limited and untrustworthy, and the wise are mum. A therapist's reputation remains in danger forever after marrying a former patient, as though people will say, "Well, she did it once; she may do it again." Marriage is taken to be an instance of having sex with a patient. The persona field is filled with landmines. Although no one will *say* anything, the marrying therapists may be painted with the same brush as sexual predators.

The cloud under which they live is another indication of our collective "complex" about sex and therapy. Although they surely know first hand more than the rest of us will ever learn about the relationship of therapy, sex, and marriage, a frightened persona-field atmosphere forces them to keep silent. The unspoken public logic seems to be that because the sexual feelings that led to their marriage *began* in therapy, the marriage itself is a kind of "acting out" of therapeutic feelings.

I have frequently heard two versions of this attitude. The first addresses a presumed self-deception: *They think it's all right as long as they marry them.* The second is prognostic: *A marriage based on transference is bound to fail.* Both arguments deny the couple's claim to be an exception to the fundamental rule of *no sex in therapy.* The first impugns the integrity of the couple, claiming "commitment" is just an excuse for "acting out." The second grants them their good intentions but dismisses them as naive.

They think it's all right as long as they marry them, means "they have convinced themselves all too easily that they can sleep with any patient they marry." The patient is always a patient. They were patients years ago in therapy, patients at the altar, and patients nursing babies. There is never an exception to the rule proscribing sex. There are only therapists who have assuaged their own dubious consciences and deluded themselves into thinking they can *create* an exception by promising to share their lives. They believe they have demonstrated their good intentions by freely choosing to stand at the altar, rendering shotguns unnecessary. They have overlooked the fact that good intentions can blind us to the greatest injustices.

A marriage based on transference is bound to fail, agrees that the patient is always a patient. It implies that the impulse to marry arises from a typically therapeutic situation, recalling the testimony of Searles that he felt married to the patients with whom he engaged most successfully. But, in contrast with Searles' writings, this attitude assumes the transference and countertransference are never resolved.

Perhaps the marriage attempts to freeze the relationship at a stage that might have been surmounted if the therapy had been allowed to run its course. Possibly nature resumes her course after the wedding, in which case the couple is rudely awakened as they discover the illusory foundation of their presumed love for one another. Then they either divorce sadly or hang on tenaciously and resentfully, unwilling to admit their mistake publicly. Alternatively it may be that transference illusions are never challenged, even in marriage, so that the couple remains forever out of balance with one another—the former patient always one-sidedly dependent, and the therapist's grandiosity flattered for life.

Both attitudes (*they think it's all right* and *marriage based on transference*) are markedly pessimistic, even cynical, about therapy and marriage, stubbornly assuming the worst of both institutions. Particularly noteworthy is the implication that no transformation is envisaged. The patient presumably never structures a self sufficiently to emerge from the lop-sided rapport of therapy's first stage. The bonding between the two parties is taken to have an insuperably regressive character—even in a marriage that lasts for decades. Apparently if the married couple believe themselves to be happy, this only proves their deludedness and immaturity. Marriage, in this view, is not an interactive field that might foster the unfolding of two selves but an eternal stasis, a petrification in the illusory fantasies that engendered it.

We have to be suspicious of such self-satisfied opinions, with their implication that anyone who is well-balanced and wise will follow the course the speaker has chosen. Possibly there is no little "narcissistic envy" and "shadow projection" in views that are so broadly belittling. Wherever individual differences have been denied, we are dealing with collective opinions whose value lies only in statistical averages. While they may serve to temper the grandiose assumption that we ourselves are an exception to every rule, we might resist the equally self-flattering tendency to assume that others are adequately addressed by such generalities. Exceptions will always arise, and they have more to teach us than the predictable and regular.

Every relationship that respects the *structure of erotic interaction*, begins by holding collective maxims in suspicion. It "brackets" everything well-known and foreseen and embarks in strategic ignorance. Surely broad experience and wide theoretical acquaintance is essential for a good therapist, but these may not be allowed to stand in the way of our perceiving and appreciating the irreplaceable uniqueness of our patient's *you*. Before the mystery of that emerging and unfolding self, we discard expectations and traditional certainties in order to be schooled through an erotic interaction with the *you* itself. In the submission and receptivity of the unitary moment, we allow the patient's *you* to affect our *I*; and in the discipline and assertiveness of the distancing moment, we enable that influence to come to consciousness and articulation.

If all this is true of a contractual relationship like therapy that works against nature, how much more will we expect open-minded "ignorance" of a spouse? Although in marriage we may not wish to call such unknowing "strategic"—lest we imply an unnatural calculating attitude—there can be little doubt that a stance of purely loving regard will be under pressure from all sides to conform to stereotyped notions. Our personal "complexes" have rigid expectations, are easily insulted, and take umbrage at the slightest misunderstanding. Furthermore, knowingly or not, we have been indoctrinated in the ideas and values of the persona world, so that we may be easily disappointed or too much impressed by certain traits in our partner. Thus marriage requires a loving ignorance no less essentially than therapy, for only unknowing susceptibility tempered with clear-sighted distance can do justice to another's *you*.

As we outlined in Chapter Six, a long-lasting sexual partnership shares as fully in the *structure of erotic interaction* as does therapy. Indeed, we speculated that the alternating and simultaneous moments of union and distance that a sexual relationship makes possible implies that a long-term committed relationship like marriage may provide the most important forum, outside of therapy, for the structuring and unfolding of nuclear selves. Marriage, too, when it is fully an erotic relationship, is founded upon an empathic love that seeks to know, articulate, and intimately engage with a *you*. The partners dissolve into a *we* and re-establish their separate sense of *I-ness* in a progressive, mutual venture of discovery that takes place not only in the intensity of love-making but also across the dinner table and over weeks and years as they raise children, pursue their individual careers, and tend to their partnership.

If therapy is notorious for its "transference phenomena," that is for the neurotic, illusory way in which unresolved issues from one's childhood are imported into the *temenos* and "projected" onto one's partner, marriage is equally freighted with expectations derived from one's parents and siblings. Both the therapeutic process and the marriage relationship are complicated by stereotyped expectations from the past and rigid hopes for the future, all of which threaten our ability to see clearly the *you* who stands before us. Both are successful only when such habitual unconscious perceptions and responses can be held sufficiently in abeyance so that the *I* and the *you* can see one another clearly through the lens of their *we*.

Therapy has been designed to recognize and bring to consciousness these habitual stereotypes. Indeed, it is generally on account of therapy's reputation for cutting through such distortions that an individual decides to devote a significant life-episode to therapeutic work. Because they affect every sector of our lifeworld—particularly, perhaps, relationships—what we take to be the "matter" of therapy intrudes into our long-term committed relationships as a set of obstacles to be recognized and set aside. Marriage brings us face-to-face with the issues we normally relegate to therapy. In fact, they intrude upon every erotic interaction as distractions and distortions that obscure our vision and prevent us from seeing the *you*, recognizing the role of our own *I*, and distinguishing the unique agency of the *we*.

Seen this way, in the context of erotic interaction, the often-heard objection, *a marriage based on transference is bound to fail*, has a very specific meaning. It implies that the therapist/patient relationship that would convert itself into a marriage has gotten stuck in the preliminary issues, the distortions brought about by unexamined complexes on both sides. For it is the failure to see, appreciate, and love one's partner for who she is and to be seen and loved in return that would cause a marriage—or any erotic interaction—to fail. If the "transference" is responsible for this, it is "a distorted, neurotic, and injurious way of seeing."

People limited by such a transference will never have faced one another in "strategic ignorance." Their therapeutic interactions will have been based upon a failure to see and be seen that made them *long for the love that had been denied them as children*. They will have wished to marry only because their therapeutic process has failed, because they have not been able to see one another clearly for who they are, and because an *I*, a *you*, and a *we* have not yet been differentiated.

No doubt many attempts at therapy (not to mention marriage) fail for precisely this reason. But must they all? Perhaps we can agree that those who have failed at the erotic interaction of therapy may well fail again if they try marriage. When the fundamental issue has not been confronted and resolved in therapy, we might doubt the individuals will find a way to deal with it as life partners. But what of those who succeed at therapy and still wish to marry? Or is it perhaps the case that those who wish to marry are inevitably the ones who failed at therapy? Is wanting to get married a symptom of therapeutic failure as well as its likely repetition? Is this what is meant by a *marriage based on transference*?

Surely one meaning of *transference* is "a relationship based upon perceptions that have been distorted by unexamined complexes." This most common variety of entanglement is often called "neurotic transference." But in the *temenos* of a clear-sighted erotic interaction, *transference* would refer to something quite different: the rapport of a self-self connection, the compelling and numinous sense of an open pathway between one's deepest identity and the unique otherness of a *you*, vibrant with well-channeled narcissistic energies, redolent of new meaning, purpose, and creativity. A third meaning of "transference" is also possible, for we are engaged in a highly exciting relationship when our narcissistic energies have broken loose from their self-synthesis and infect both parties so as to produce a *dissolving* mystical participation. This last possibility can be so crazily compelling that it is sometimes called "psychotic transference."

Because *transference* has so many meanings, the notion of a *marriage based on transference* ought to be an equally broad category. No doubt there are those who attempt to achieve in marriage a satisfaction that has been denied them in their therapeutic interaction, in the sense of a search for the *love they had longed for as children*. In their compulsive longing, if a therapist who has still not glimpsed their emerging self nevertheless seems willing to love them, and if the unitive moment of their erotic interaction seems to promise a wonderful future, they are probably eager to repeat the frustration they experienced in childhood.

But if therapy is a love cure, if the erotic channels are open, if an *I* and a *you* maintain a clear-eyed distance amid their union in a *we*, then the therapy itself would supply the empathic regard they have longed for all their lives. If, beyond this, their self has gained coherent structure and the erotic *temenos* has been the arena for the unfolding of their personal myth, the wish to marry their therapist will have a rather different meaning. We may still call this a *marriage based on transference*, but we will have an entirely different prognosis of the committed partnership they envisage than we would have for a couple whose transference is characterized by the blindness of unresolved complexes or the corrosive effects of unchanneled narcissistic energies.

The ethical considerations incumbent upon a therapist who is contemplating marriage with a patient will be very much the same as those we detailed in Chapter Seven. Ultimately, through a detailed investigation of the therapeutic interaction, the therapist would have to arrive at an intelligently skeptical assessment of the three agents in the process: the two selves and the *we*. The central question would concern the significance of their erotic interaction for the unfolding of these three centers. Can the interaction they are engaged in be adequately designated as *therapy*, i.e., as a paradigmatic episode in the triple unfolding, where the *we* has come to presence and begun to unfold as a kind of lesson or exemplary model for the unfolding of their individual selves? Or is it rather that this unfolding process is so significant that it cannot be relegated to the role of an episode in their respective lifeworlds but must be embraced as a joint life-long commitment?

If therapist and patient decide upon the latter alternative, their critics may feel justified in claiming, *they think it's all right as long as they marry them.* They *do* think it will be all right if they marry, but not as a sort of legitimation for sexual "acting out." They have decided, rather, that their erotic interaction cannot be confined by the limited and episodic nature of therapy to assist in the unfolding of their selves. The work they have begun in therapy has grown into the central work of their respective lives. They do not truncate the therapeutic work to enjoy the pleasures of sex. They expand that work into every corner of their lives. They act not from lust but from the embodiment of Eros' distance-amid-union.

It need hardly be emphasized that the decision to marry a patient would be open to profound suspicion if it occurred more than once in a therapist's lifetime. Furthermore, we might expect that within the population of therapists, decisions to marry patients would be relatively rare. The latter expectation has probably not been met, as unofficial estimates suggest that twenty to twenty-five percent of therapists may be married to former patients. Because another sizable percentage of therapists is married to other therapists, we might conservatively estimate that a third to a half of the therapist population is married to partners who have had significant experience with the *structure of erotic interaction* in the concentrated, episodic format of therapy. When we add to this the fact that another large portion of the therapist population is unmarried, we might possibly conclude that people who spend the greater portion of their professional lives in erotic *temenoi* will not be satisfied with a partner who is unfamiliar with relationship in which distance-amid-union plays a central role.

The two common dismissals of marriages between therapists and patients miss the point by failing to take Eros into consideration. They thereby underestimate both therapy and marriage. No doubt many therapists and many spouses do the same having attained little or no critical distance from the assumptions of the persona field. Probably there are many marrying therapists who do *think it's all right as long as they marry them* and many whose *marriage based on* (unresolved) *transference* issues *fails*. These will be the casualties of an insufficient recognition of the erotic nature of both therapy and marriage.

The ethical dogmatism of the persona field may have an instructive effect on those who are unaware of deeper realities. If so, the maxims serve a useful purpose. It seems likely to me, however, that therapists who get to the point of imagining marriage with a specific patient must have caught a glimpse of Eros' potential to open up the self field. If so, their dilemma will not be adequately addressed by a perspective on therapy that does not take the *structure of erotic interaction* prominently into its calculations.

Conclusion

Frustration, Optimal
and Depreciating

It may seem that I am proposing a very dangerous approach to psychotherapy. In place of the persona field's overriding interest in making
the erotic dimension of therapy safer by setting up "boundaries" and
observing them with a sense of heroic, moral superiority, I have argued that it is the erotic itself that effects the transformations
psychotherapy seeks. Consequently "the erotic" ought to be not so
much controlled as observed.

One of my colleagues goes so far as to recommend the image of
Odysseus who lashes himself to the mast of his ship as he passes the
island of the Sirens. He permits himself to hear the erotic song that is
famous for drawing men to their destruction but has stopped the ears
of his sailors with wax and ordered them in advance to row
unswervingly despite whatever his Siren-caused madness may pro-
pose. This may surely seem to be an image of "bearing the tension" of
a powerfully sexual countertransference. The iron will of his ego lashes
itself to the maxims of the persona field so that his patient's siren
song cannot divert him from his ethical course despite the pull toward erotic and sexual union he fears he lacks the strength to resist.

Noble as it is, there is a problem with this image. If the Sirens represent the unchanneled narcissistic energies stirred by the patient's
incoherent self, infecting the therapist with an irresistible impulse to

"sexual acting out," the therapist is not merely Odysseus. He is also those sailors with their ears plugged. The scene from the *Odyssey*, therefore, proposes an image of a therapist who is pathologically split. He hears but acts as though he does not, conveying a mixed message to his patient. He brands her voice demonic, destructive, and evil. He frustrates her demand for inappropriate narcissistic gratification, all right, but by no means "optimally." He fails to respond to and "mirror" her emerging self.

Although "righteous" and "ethical" in a way the persona field would surely approve, he has converted an opportunity for "optimal frustration" into a "depreciating frustration." Instead of structuring her self, he confirms its incoherence and contributes to the obliteration of any emerging structure that might have been discerned in her "sexualized" desire to dissolve in the *we*. Furthermore, by lashing himself righteously to the mast of his respectable therapeutic persona, he implicitly asserts that the madness and incoherence is all hers. He is the virtuous and healthy one. She is destructive, infectious, and evil. This publicly approved frustration depreciates her as the hopelessly deranged Siren she fears she is.

His lashing himself to the mast is an act of fear that subverts the *structure of erotic interaction* just as surely as lust. For while lust would truncate the erotic tension by yielding to the unitive impulse, "depreciating frustration" truncates it by anxious repudiation and flight. In lust the tension collapses, in flight it flies apart.

Above all, what is fled in a truncated encounter of this type, is the therapist's own participation in a *temenos* filled with unchanneled narcissistic energies. In lashing ourselves to the mast, we disavow that the madness is *ours*. But it is precisely *as ours*, as a mutual reality between ourselves and our patient, that it affects us. We would not need to exert such extraordinary efforts to restrain ourselves from a madness belonging to our patient, alone. The lashing is therefore a lie that, as such, no doubt repeats all the abandoning and depreciating frustrations of our patient's life. Once again *she* is the one who is unworthy of relatedness. Once again the *you* with whom she hopes for a healing and transformative encounter, by whom she might be valued as the emerging self she is, repudiates her.

Peter Rutter presents a much more useful model for dealing with a difficult and sexualized encounter, although it also is too much conditioned by the persona field's confusion of "the erotic" with "the sexual." He calls the refusal to participate sexually with the patient "the healing moment," and defines it as follows: "Whenever a man relinquishes his sexual agenda toward his protege in order to preserve her right to a nonsexual relationship, a healing moment occurs" (Rutter, 1989, p. 250).

The crucial phrase in this definition is *in order to preserve her right to a nonsexual relationship*. Insofar as the therapist looks to his patient's "rights," and indeed to her identity, he bases his refusal on who she is *in herself*, as a unique and irreplaceable *you*, an emerging or unfolding self. He "mirrors" at the same time that he frustrates, and demonstrates in the process his emotional involvement in a mutual concern. His refusal is an instance of "optimal frustration." Although Rutter's book never uses such language or articulates such a point of view, it is clear that he has grasped the essential matter. "Optimal frustration," by whatever name, frustrates "optimally" and proceeds from empathy, the erotic way of loving that holds the tension of distance-amid-union.

Surely everyone has a *right to a nonsexual relationship*, and any coercion or taking advantage would be not only a violation of that right but a denial of the individual's identity as well. The problem with this formulation, however, is that it assumes that a *need* for a nonsexual relationship is always definitive of the patient. It starts out from the absolute position of the persona field that presumes—and never explores or intelligently doubts—that sexual relating is always the wrong thing to do. It closes the question of sexuality by beginning with an *a priori* concept of the patient's identity. It never accepts her sexual presentation of herself as a valid and valuable expression of her emerging nuclear self.

Very likely the inappropriateness of sexual enactment will turn out to be verified in the vast majority of cases. But an *a priori* attitude does not allow for the possibility that this particular unique individual may be an exception to the general run of patients. It stuffs her into a pigeon-hole labeled "patient in need of protection from her sexual self." In this one respect, sexuality, my patient is not allowed to be a unique individual but must conform to public expectations.

There may be one in several million patients for whom a sexual relationship with the therapist would be supported by the unfolding of both selves and the *we*—successful marriages between them being an instance. But there is surely a much larger number who sincerely believe their relationship with their therapist is an exception to the universal rule. I have seen several of these people in my practice, individuals whose work with another therapist was suddenly terminated because the sexual energy became too strong for the therapist to bear. Although I am not inclined to believe that any of the patients were right in their conviction that the therapist should have acceded to their sexual requests, the abrupt termination prevented an exploration that might have uncovered the difference between Eros and sexuality and elucidated the emerging self that seemed to desire it.

The love cure is a more difficult way, possibly a more dangerous way, but it is the only way to give full attention and respect to the unique emerging and unfolding self of the patient. In this more fundamental sense, it is a *less* dangerous way. Surely it seems dangerous to leave open the question of sexual enactment. But the requirements for dealing with *any* open question in the context of the love cure are highly complex and reduce the danger to manageable moment-by-moment evaluations through an intelligent and empathic skepticism which holds open the tension between what we think we want and what the *we* wants of us.

There may be times when a therapist of the love cure discovers her own coherence in the realm of sexuality may not be up to the task of holding open the question of sexual enactment. If so, the love cure hardly requires that she persist in the face of likely failure. But at the same time, the possibility of "optimal frustration" is by no means excluded. If termination seems imperative, as the only way to avoid truncating the *structure of erotic interaction* by "sexual acting out," this, too, can be done empathically. Rather than lashing herself to the mast of her respectability and leaving her patient to bear the burden of the pathology, she will be required by empathy to lay out the state of affairs honestly, sharing with sorrow and fear her own confusion.

Perhaps this in itself will be enough to alter the sexually charged atmosphere and allow the love cure to proceed. But even if it does not, even if there is no way out aside from referring the patient to another therapist, this, too, can be done in the spirit of the love cure. The essential stance of empathy requires seeing and articulating the patient's emerging self as clearly and honestly as possible and with full emotional vulnerability. This will necessarily entail sharing the madness as *ours*. If the termination and referral are not experienced as a stoic repudiation but as a loving and affirming guidance, the emerging self will be "mirrored" and frustrated empathically.

In this sense, termination itself may become an "optimal frustration," even though every terrified impulse in the therapist's psyche wants to flee to safety and hide behind a self-righteous and depreciating frustration.

Appendix

Summary of the Argument

When therapy is recognized as essentially erotic, that is, as structured by a tripartite tension between an *I*, a *you*, and a *we*, the participants find themselves drawn into a compelling dissolution that promises an enlargement filled with meaning-giving and energizing narcissistic possibilities. Their desire to dissolve may even be experienced sexually, in the sense that they may hope a sexual enactment will unite them in a rapturous experience of all they can be, everything their past has been leading up to. At the same time, they fear what it will do to their habitual sense of who they have been; for to dissolve the only identity they have known faces them with the prospect of personal annihilation. The inauthentic sexual enactment of lust would destroy the *we* and the *you* by annexing the *you* as a set of qualities I would make my own. At the other extreme, fear and its ally, rage, would repudiate the *we* and the *you* in order to preserve myself.

The *structure of erotic interaction*, therefore, requires that the tension between dissolving and preserving be maintained. In therapy this means that the therapist is called upon to assume a stance of distance-amid-union. The unitive moment is experienced in the pull of the *we* toward dissolution. The distancing moment is expressed in assuming an observer's attitude, whereby the *I*, the *you*, and the *we* can be appreciated as three distinct participants in the process. Kohut has named this tension-holding stance "empathy."

Empathy by its very nature responds to another. The reality of the *you* whom I encounter takes precedence over all guidelines and pre-suppositions. The *you* calls for recognition, "mirroring," and "optimal frustration," three activities that cannot be specified in advance as to "content." Only the *you* determines *what* is recognized, mirrored, and frustrated; and every *you* is a unique and irreplaceable person. What is most essential to empathy can be found only separately in each individual case. The "content" of an empathic response is always determined in and through the encounter itself.

Furthermore, empathy is a *loving* response. Here, "loving" does not mean gushing, romanticizing, or servitude. Empathy is loving in the sense of *the love they had longed for as children*, i.e., a love that sees them for the unique emerging self they are. In this sense, empathy is a sober, reality-oriented way of seeing. It sees what is really there, the emerging/unfolding self of the *you*.

And it is *my* seeing. Although a particular *you* is there to be seen by anyone who encounters it, it is in each case encountered by a unique *I*. My empathic response to *you* calls upon my distinct and irrepeatable self-hood. As a flowing forth and expression of my central identity, it is the response that only *I* can give. My empathic response to you is vibrant with my spontaneous emotionality, even as I describe your emerging self with an accuracy proper to my own unique perspective. It is a kind of giving of myself, for it is the heartfelt gesture my self makes as a salute and rejoinder to the presence of the *you*.

This seeing and being seen, loving and being loved occurs in a space that sets itself apart from the world-at-large. It is defined by our meeting, the shared encounter that mingles *me* with *you* in the third reality we call the *we*. Empathy is the seeing and responding that occurs in our *we*, in which neither of us is strictly speaking an "object" for the other. Each of us is a subjectivity, a self that emerges or unfolds within the gaze of the other's empathy, the other's ability to see us through the lens of the *we*. Our selves are mutually implicated and entangled in that *we*, so that what happens to either of us affects the other.

Appendix: Summary of the Argument

The *we* is that process of our mutual influence upon one another through empathic engagement. As such, it stands over against both of us as a third reality which somehow sums up our mutuality but is still *other than* either of us. Our *I* and *you* come to understand themselves and one another in the context of the *we*, this mysterious reality portentous of our mutual future and guiding our interaction. The process of being guided by the *we* is definitive of empathy and the ground of the love cure. It is the life of Eros, the tripartite engagement that establishes therapy's *temenos* and sets its agenda.

To talk like this to describe therapy from the *inside*, as a kind of loving engagement whose features can never be specified in advance of the process itself. What is called for by the empathic interaction of this unique *I* and *you*, emerges in and only in their unique encounter. Only the most general features can be mentioned, namely that a pair of emerging or unfolding selves are mutually seen, accurately described, and optimally frustrated. We can also categorize these encounters in a general way into two types: those which involve a patient with an unstructured and incoherent self, where an unbalanced emerging self/self-object bond obtains between therapist and patient, and those which involve a patient with a relatively structured and coherent self, where patient and therapist enjoy a self-self bond that is more evenly balanced.

We summarize the work expected of these two kinds of therapy by saying that in the former the patient's self requires "structuring," while in the latter it requires "unfolding." These are the grossest kind of shorthand notation. But unfortunately we can say little more, for the work of structuring and unfolding is in each case unique. Its requirements are established within the therapeutic *temenos*, where the agenda is set by the *we* that comes to presence between this particular therapist and patient.

To say the work takes place within a *temenos* is to emphasize the "innerness" of the tripartite erotic process, the fact that it takes place between an *I*, a *you*, and a *we* in an interpersonal space that is "cut off" (*temno* = "I cut") from the world-at-large, where public expectations hold sway. The love cure follows the guidance of the *we* and respects the requirements that emerge from this process *inside* the encounter itself.

Because of this "cut off" quality belonging to every therapeutic *temenos*, the love cure, which takes place only within and by means of *temenoi* grounded in a *we*, arouses the suspicions of a public world that is concerned with ethical propositions that are necessarily generalized broadly enough to apply to everyone. Such generalized maxims are by no means without merit. Indeed they summarize the experience of millions of individuals and have the force and wisdom of a consensus. Nevertheless, as public and generalized, they represent the world outside the therapeutic *temenos*.

Consequently, for the *I* and the *you* inside the *temenos*, such maxims represent propositions extrinsic to the encounter. Because of their consensual power, they deserve the most careful consideration. But still, as extrinsic to the *temenos*, they are not above intelligent, skeptical investigation. Indeed, the primacy of the *we* requires that they be doubted.

This generates a good deal of suspicious tension between the love cure and the ethical sensibilities of the public world. The latter promulgates absolute rules, such as, *any aspect of sex in the context of therapy is always wrong*, in order to establish safety and dependability. Such a maxim sets the laudable goal of making therapy a profession in which the rapacity of renegade therapists is securely outlawed.

Although no conscientious therapist could ever doubt the appropriateness of such an aim, the therapist of the love cure is required by the *structure of erotic interaction* to doubt the absoluteness of such maxims in order to remain faithful to the primacy of the *we*. The love-cure therapist hardly doubts that sexuality is a dangerous and unreliable adjunct to therapy and expects to pursue a therapeutic career without violating this persona-field proposition.

But the fact that the love-cure may not subordinate the primacy of the *we* to the absolute maxims of the public world, means that the love cure itself is liable to be held in suspicion by the persona field and the majority of the population that takes its guidance from such generalized laws. These suspicions are an unfortunate reality, particularly in view of the fact that the love cure, by its very nature, is a highly ethical endeavor.

Taking its guidance from the *we* and the emerging or unfolding self of the *you*, the love cure is obliged in each moment to further the coherence and assist the unfolding of that *you*. In no case may any casual experimentation or ego-centered self-promotion be allowed to interfere with the therapeutic *structure of erotic interaction*. This, in itself, assures that the love cure cannot countenance "sexual acting out," in the sense of an arbitrary pursuit of pleasure or power.

Nevertheless the love cure is consistent in its refusal to subordinate its empathic concern with the self of the patient to the absolute rules of the persona field. If it suffers some lack of public respect on this account, it also offers two significant assets over an approach to therapy which would disregard the *structure of erotic interaction* in order to remain comfortably in harmony with publicly approved values. (a) It affirms the uniqueness of the patient's *you*, maintaining an attitude of "strategic ignorance" whereby all attempts to define the identity of the patient in advance are rejected in favor of the patient's own manifestation of a unique emerging and unfolding self. (b) By leaving all questions open for intelligent skepticism within the *temenos* of the *we*, it explores regions of individual and interpersonal experience that are prematurely closed off by an *a priori* acceptance of public dogma.

Because the love cure is that mode of therapy which responds to and conforms itself with the *structure of erotic interaction*, and because Eros is present whenever two individuals meet in such a way as to take one another seriously as a distinct *I* and a distinct *you* who matter so much to one another that they are mutually involved in a *we*, we conclude that every form of therapy that understands the centrality and depth of this involvement will be a love cure, whether or not the therapist and patient have developed the language to articulate it. Deeply and essentially understood, every therapy is a love cure. Consequently, any attempt to close off questions that arise within the *temenos* of the *we* fails as therapy. This is true regardless of the therapist's intention in closing the question—whether out of a desire to conform to the assumptions of a public consensus or out of an inability or fear of holding the tension.

Therapy's failure is always a failure of empathy, the loving attitude of distance-amid-union. Failures of empathy, at least of a momentary kind, are inevitable in every therapeutic process—and indeed in every erotic relationship. Therapy itself fails only when these momentary empathic lapses are not addressed in a subsequent interchange characterized by empathy. The patient will experience such lapses as injurious misunderstandings, and they will give the therapist sufficient feedback to know something is wrong and eventually to recognize them as failures. Humble, honest, and emotionally vulnerable acknowledgment of the patient's injury and the therapist's own responsibility for it constitutes the only response that is truly empathic and appropriate. As an empathic response, it turns failure into opportunity, an "optimal frustration."

Thus, as it lurches along through empathic successes, failures, and optimal frustrations, the love cure follows the guidance of the *we*, wherein every success is *ours*, every failure is *ours*, and what we may yet achieve advances before us like an opening horizon of mutual possibility. The *we* is actualized in every mutual interaction we conduct. It thereby becomes more real and definite as we proceed and reveals to us in the form of intimations the path its unfolding is opening for us.

Bibliography

Publication dates which appear in the form, 1920/58, provide both the date of the first version of the work (1920) and the latest revision (1958). References to the *Collected Works* of C. G. Jung (Princeton University Press; translated by R. F. C. Hull) are indicated by CW followed by the volume number.

Anonymous, "Psychiatrists and Sex Abuse." (1994). The Boston *Globe*, Tuesday, October 4.

Baker, N., *Vox*. (1992). New York: Random House.

Buber, M., *Daniel: Dialogues on Realization*. (1965). (Tr. M. Friedman). New York: McGraw-Hill.

Carotenuto, A., *A Secret Symmetry*. (1982). New York: Pantheon.

Donleavy, P., "Analysis and Erotic Energies." *The Interactive Field in Analysis, Volume I*, (1995) Willmette, IL, Chiron: 107-121

Haule, J. R., "'Soul-making' in a Schizophrenic Saint." (1984). *Journal of Religion and Health* 23(1): 70-80.

Haule, J. R., "Pierre Janet and Dissociation: The First Transference Theory and Its Origins in Hypnosis," (1986). *American Journal of Hypnosis* 29(2): 86-94.

Haule, J. R., *Divine Madness: Archetypes of Romantic Love*. (1990). Boston: Shambhala. Paperback title, *Pilgrimage of the Heart: The Path of Romantic Love*. (1992). Boston: Shambhala.

Haule, J. R., "Erotic Analysis and the Shape of Eros." (1995a). *Spring 57*, 73-88.

Haule, J. R., "Eros, Mutuality, and the 'New Ethic'" (1995b). Ross and Roy, (1995), 9-15

Janet, P., *Automatisme psychologique*. (1889). *Paris: Société Pierre Janet*, 1973.

Janet, P., *De l'anguisse à l'extase*. 2 Vols. (1926). Paris: *Société Pierre Janet*, 1975.

John of the Cross. *The Collected Works*. (1979). Translated by K. Kavanaugh & O. Rodriguez. Washington, D.C.: Institute of Carmelite Studies.

Jung, C. G., *Symbols of Transformation: An Analysis of the Prelude to a Case of Schizophrenia*. (1912/52). *CW 5*.

Jung, C. G., "The Structure of the Unconscious." (1916). CW 7, 269-304.

Jung, C. G., "A Study in the Process of Individuation" (1934/50). CW 9i, 290-354.

Jung, C. G., *Psychology and Alchemy* (1944/52). CW 12.

Jung, C. G., *The Psychology of the Transference*. (1946). CW 16, 163-323.

Jung, C. G., *Memories, Dreams, Reflections*. (1961). Recorded and edited by A. Jaffe. Translated by R. & C. Winston. New York: Pantheon.

Jung, C. G., *Two Essays in Analytical Psychology*. (1966). CW 7.

Kerr, J., *A Most Dangerous Method*. (1993). New York: Knopf.

Kohut, H., *The Analysis of the Self*. (1971). New York: International Universities.

Kohut, H., *The Restoration of the Self*. (1977). New York: International Universities.

Kohut, H., *How Does Analysis Cure?* (1984). Chicago: University of Chicago.

Kohut, H., *Self Psychology and the Humanities*. (1985). New York: Norton.

McGuire, W., (Ed.). *The Freud/Jung Letters*. (1974). Princeton: Princeton University Press.

Pike, N., *Mystic Union: An Essay in the Phenomenology of Mysticism*. (1992). Ithaca: Cornell.

Roazen, P., *Freud and His Followers*. (1976). New York: Knopf.

Ross, L. B., and M. Roy (Eds.). *Cast the First Stone: Ethics in Analytical Practice*. (1995). Chicago: Chiron.

Rutter, P., *Sex in the Forbidden Zone*. (1989). Los Angeles: Tarcher.

Searles, H., "Oedipal Love in the Countertransference" (1959). In *Collected Papers on Schizophrenia and Related Subjects*. International Universities, 1965.

Teresa of Avila. *The Interior Castle*. (1979). Translated by K. Kavanaugh & O. Rodriguez. New York: Paulist.

Psychology for the 21st Century

Pagan Meditations • Ginette Paris

Montreal's well known psychologist, Ginette Paris, began her studies in women's psychology with this book. It has become a foundation—nothing less—for the study of goddesses (Aphrodite, Artemis and Hestia) and how they fit into women's lives today. "I found myself wanting to read this one out loud to anyone listening."—Utne Reader

204 pp. ISBN 0-88214-330-1

Impossible Love: or Why the Heart Must Go Wrong • Jan Bauer

Some love affairs mark our lives forever, remaining indelible because impossible. This brilliant work explores the nature of these "marvelous disasters" and finds a deeper necessity in the betrayals, taboos and excesses of impossible love. Using perhaps the greatest of all tragic romances—the passion between Heloise and Abelard—Jan Bauer examines the erotic structures of irresistible attraction with love stories from the lives of men and women today.

207 pp. ISBN 0-88214-359-X

Dark Eros: The Imagination of Sadism • Thomas Moore

What is the author of the best-sellers Care of the Soul and Soul Mates doing with this shocking subject—writing on the hidden values in the fascinating and erotic fictions of the Marquis de Sade? Moore offers a fearlessly new reading of sadism as he exposes the psychological and imaginative implications of torture, violence and victimization. He tries to open a way through the cruelties that affect family, education, love affairs and work. A must for Moore fans!

200 pp. ISBN 0-88214-365-4

From the Wrong Side:
A Paradoxical Approach to Psychology • Adolf Guggenbühl-Craig
Translated by Gary V. Hartman

This long-awaited book from the popular author of Power in the Helping Professions and Eros on Crutches, exposes the hidden hypocrisies of conventional psychology by looking at the profession from a refreshing and paradoxical point of view. By deliberately taking the "wrong side" of many politically and psychologically "correct" positions, this former head of the Jung Institute in Zürich brings new light and ideas to a profession that seems to become more stuck and bland everyday. Includes a commentary by Sidney Handel on "The Work and Thought of Adolf Guggenbühl-Craig."

165 pp. ISBN 0-88214-357-3

Power in the Helping Professions • Adolf Guggenbühl-Craig

Find out why Power in the Helping Professions is required reading for counselors and therapists around the world. In this concise book, Guggenbühl-Craig, a therapist for more than 50 years, teaches us how to be aware of the subtle abuses of authority that can occur during therapy. Everyone has been on both sides of power-manipulation relationships, but without an objective method, becoming aware of these occurrences is difficult if not impossible. "In a nation where subconscious sado-masochism between psychologist and patient is a cultural cliché, this book is a...starting point for change."—CoEVOLUTION Quarterly

155 pp. ISBN 0-88214-304-2

for a free catalog, write:
Spring Publications, Inc.
299 East Quassett Road, Woodstock, CT 06281
or call (860) 974-3428
visit our website at: http://www.neca.com/~spring